The New Americans
Recent Immigration and American Society

Edited by
Steven J. Gold and Rubén G. Rumbaut

A Series from LFB Scholarly

Mexican Migrants and their Parental Households in Mexico

Paula Fomby

LFB Scholarly Publishing LLC
New York 2005

Copyright © 2005 by LFB Scholarly Publishing LLC

Library of Congress Cataloging-in-Publication Data

Fomby, Paula.
  Mexican migrants and their parental households in Mexico / Paula
Fomby.
      p. cm. -- (The new Americans)
  Includes bibliographical references and index.
  ISBN 1-59332-074-4 (alk. paper)
  1. Mexico--Emigration and immigration. 2. Mexicans--United States--
Family relationships. 3. Emigrant remittances--Mexico--Sociological
aspects. 4. Households--Mexico. 5. Migrant labor--United States. I.
Title. II. Series: New Americans (LFB Scholarly Publishing LLC)
  JV7402.F65 2005
    306.85'0972--dc22

2005021179

ISBN 1-59332-074-4

Printed on acid-free 250-year-life paper.

Manufactured in the United States of America.

CONTENTS

TABLES AND FIGURES

CHAPTER 1

Introduction
Households of Origin and Mexico-U.S. Migration

The history of Mexican migration to the United States has been recorded and theorized as a story about male labor migration. The economic and sociological models derived from a focus on male migrants assume that the objectives of migration are to facilitate nuclearization by establishing separate households and to improve the standard of living in families of procreation. But to look at migrants only from this perspective presents a truncated view that captures migrants in the middle of their careers, after they have become spouses and parents.

Research considering migrants at the midpoint of their careers typically overlooks them as involved members of the families in which they grew up. As a result, relatively little is known about how migrants participate in systems of intergenerational relations and exchange with parents and siblings. But the households where children grow up are a critical source of social and financial capital that young adults use as they begin to migrate. After initiating migration, young adults influence the supply of instrumental and financial assistance available to parents and siblings by altering the composition of the parental household and by providing remittances as a source of income.

This book is designed to address the issues of how adult children, parents, and siblings in Mexico relate to each other in the context of international migration. Specifically, it considers how parental households enable or constrain the inception of Mexican-U.S. migration by young adults, and how migration by children in early adulthood functions to sustain parental households in Mexico.

The volume of migration to the United States by young adults from Mexico, the economic position of households in contemporary Mexico, and changes in the composition of migrant flows speak to the importance of understanding young migrants in their parents' households. On the first point, a significant segment of Mexico's migrants are young adults who would be expected to have active ties to their families of origin. Of the approximately 300,000 Mexican men and women who migrate to the United States annually,[1] twenty-seven percent are between 18 and 25 years old. Almost three-quarters of these young migrants are unmarried, and 69 percent do not maintain independent households in Mexico (El Programa Paisano del Gobierno de Mexico 2001).[2] This profile suggests that young migrants are likely still engaged socially and economically with kin in the context of the parental household, as the beneficiaries of household-based social and financial capital in order to begin the trip, as providers of remittances to fuel the household economy, and as repositories of new social capital that siblings may draw on to migrate in the future.

Second, many households in Mexico lack long-term economic stability because of widespread job insecurity and an incomplete public safety net. As a result, household members rely on informal economic and instrumental support from kin. For aging parents who lack a

---

[1] The cited data source reported figures from 2000. More recent figures from the U.S. Immigration and Naturalization Service estimate that 400,000 Mexican migrants enter the United States annually (Immigration and Naturalization Service 2003).

[2] The observed low rates of marriage and headship among young migrants may represent a selection effect. That is, children who are unmarried and who do not have separate households may be better able to migrate than their married and/or household-head counterparts in Mexico because they have fewer responsibilities that tie them to their community of origin. In that case, young, unmarried Mexican adults would be overrepresented in the United States compared to their prevalence in Mexico.

pension or health insurance, adult children provide a critical source of income as well as assistance in food preparation, health care, transportation, and home maintenance. In younger households, children's employment helps to diversify sources of household income and to make the household a net source of production, rather than consumption. Children may remain physically connected to the parental household as coresidents, or they may provide support from separate households or, in the case of migrants, from the other side of an international border, where they accumulate remittances to transfer to their parents' household economy.

Third, the composition of migrant flows has changed in the last half-century in response to U.S. immigration policy, urbanization and increased women's labor force participation in Mexico, and a social context described by the cumulative causation of migration, in which each additional migration experience in a community increases the likelihood of movement by other potential migrants (Massey, Durand, and Malone 2002; Myrdal 1957). Since 1965, U.S. immigration policy has increasingly favored family reunification and the admission of highly skilled immigrants and has aggressively discouraged undocumented entry to the United States. As a result legal entrants to the United States are now mostly women (Jasso, Massey, Rosenzweig, and Smith 2000). The volume of undocumented migration has not diminished in response to increased border controls and punitive actions against employers who hire workers without the proper papers.

Although the modal category of migrants continues to be rural men, women and urban residents have become more likely to migrate in recent years. These changes affect parental households in two ways. First, migration by women implies migration by daughters, in addition to and perhaps instead of by sons. The consequences of daughters' migration for household organization, in terms of membership, economic contributions, and instrumental aid are potentially distinctive compared to the consequences of sons' migration as a result of gender-based household roles. Second, urban households in Mexico, which may themselves be the product of internal migration from rural areas, must adapt to a new form of economic organization that relies less on a coresident members' employment in the secondary sector and more on remittances.

Migrant children's remittances potentially make significant contributions to levels of economic support and productivity in parental households, but there is little data on how often remittances are transferred to parents, rather than to spouses or children. Overall in 2003, migrants to the United States remitted over $13 billion to Mexico (Federal Reserve Bank of Dallas 2004), and remittances were second only to oil exports as a source of Mexico's foreign revenue. Historically, about 70 percent of migrants have remitted earnings to their families (Massey, Durand, and Malone 2002), and receiving families use these funds both for immediate consumption and for investment in private enterprises (Durand, Parrado, and Massey 1996). If even ten percent of total remittances reach parental households, the added income would be a significant contribution for household economies lacking access to pension systems and well-functioning credit markets.

This book is laid out in seven chapters. The current chapter provides an overview of the history of Mexican migration to the United States and situates the Mexican parental household as an economic and social unit in the migration process. The second chapter summarizes the dominant theories pertaining to the separate research areas of international migration and household functioning, and considers how these two literatures might intersect to explain the role of children's migration in the parental household. The next four chapters present empirical research on questions pertaining to the relationship between the parental household and migrant children. The empirical research is based on statistical analyses of two rich, publicly available data sources developed specifically for the study of Mexico-U.S. migration. Chapter 3 describes the data sources. Chapter 4 considers the household resources children draw on to become international migrants, and asks what conditions in the household prompt some children to become migrants while their siblings remain in Mexico. The conditions that lead to the initiation of migration have been widely investigated, but the current study contributes to this body of research by modeling the explicit differences in the initiation of migration experienced by men and women and by urban and rural migrants.

Chapters 5 and 6 assess the effects of children's migration on the parents and siblings who remain in Mexico. Chapter 5 considers the structure of migrant-sending households in comparison to households with no migrant children. Specifically, the research asks whether children's migration is associated with a prolonged period of consolidation in the parental household, where family members work together to maintain the household as an economically productive unit, or with an accelerated process of dispersion, where all children leave the parental household early. Chapter 6 asks whether households with children in the United States are more likely to receive cash transfers from children. The final chapter summarizes the findings from the empirical research and discusses the implications for parental households in Mexico with U.S.-bound migrant children.

THE HISTORY OF MEXICO-U.S. MIGRATION

Mexican migration to the United States has been a part of the binational landscape since the border between the two countries was solidified in 1853. International migration followed the transformation of local economies by capitalism both in Mexico and in the United States, driven largely by the development of the railroad system. In the late nineteenth-century American southwest, the railroad was both conveyor and symbol of capitalism: its construction created an unprecedented demand for manual wage labor, and its utility spurred large-scale production and the expansion of markets. Railroad construction within Mexico also had significant repercussions for migration. The Porfirio Diaz regime encouraged rapid railroad development in the early years of the twentieth century, a project that indirectly led to the consolidation of many small family farms into a few *haciendas* producing commercial crops that could be transported and distributed quickly. This economic restructuring produced a surplus of free labor, and newly displaced *jornaleros*[3] traveled north on the rail lines in stages, eventually reaching and crossing the American border in pursuit of work (Sanchez 1993). The nature of the transformation of Mexico's economy, the traditional absence of Mexican women from the formal labor force, and the character of the manual labor available in the United States created a migrant flow dominated by young men. Despite changes in U.S. immigration policy, the urbanization of Mexico, and women's entry into the Mexican labor force, the demographics of the migration flow remained largely unchanged through most of the twentieth century (Durand, Massey, and Zenteno 2001).

---

[3] Itinerant day laborers, typically employed in the farming sector.

During the last century, private citizens, businesses, and local and national governments in the United States have alternately offered tolerant and hostile welcomes to Mexican immigrants. In the early twentieth century, economic and social conditions in the United States influenced both public opinion about immigration and the volume of Mexican-U.S. migration. Government and private business in the United States tolerated and even encouraged undocumented Mexican migration during the 1920's, even as federal policy became increasingly nativist and explicitly excluded immigrants from China.

Mexican migration declined in response to the Depression, but after entering World War II, the United States developed its first formal migration policy toward Mexico in the form of the *bracero* program. Beginning in 1942, Mexican men were allowed entry to the United States to work in the agricultural sector, which had been depleted of manual labor as American men joined the armed forces. The *bracero* program was designed as a solution to a short-term labor shortage, but after the war's end, the U.S. economy began to shift away from agriculture, and rural areas remained short-handed. As a result, the program remained in effect until 1964. Through the *bracero* program, a generation of Mexican men were exposed to the process of migration, and began the accumulation of social capital that fed the next generation of migrants.

Since 1965, U.S. policy has favored family reunification and the recruitment of skilled labor as the rationales for admitting legal immigrants, and since 1968, the number of visas offered to Mexicans has been subject to an annual cap.[4] At the same time that legal entry to the United States became more restrictive, population growth and economic uncertainty in Mexico put pressure on the national labor force to find other avenues for employment. In response, undocumented migration by Mexicans to the United States boomed in the late 1970's and early 1980's, although most migrants eventually returned to Mexico (Massey and Singer 1995). By the middle of the

---

[4] Beginning in 1968, Mexicans competed with residents of other Latin American and Caribbean countries for a total of 120,000 visas available annually in the western hemisphere. Beginning in 1976, Mexico and all countries in the western hemisphere became subject to an annual cap of 20,000 visas per country, excluding immediate relatives of U.S. citizens.

1980's, public opinion in the United States perceived undocumented migration as a social and economic problem, and federal legislators strived to create an enforceable policy of deterrence. The result was the 1986 Immigration Reform and Control Act (IRCA).

IRCA offered amnesty and legal status to undocumented migrants who could prove that they had resided in the United States for at least five years. The act was intended to make undocumented migration less attractive both to employers and to potential migrants by increasing penalties on employers who hired undocumented workers and by increasing border patrol operations. Despite significant investments in border patrol and workplace enforcement, IRCA has been ineffective in curtailing the volume of undocumented migration in the face of what had become a self-sustaining social process (Donato, Durand, and Massey 1992). However, the increased border control associated with IRCA has influenced the duration of undocumented migrants' trips, the composition of undocumented migrant flows, and the distribution of points of entry to the United States. Greater border control has not diminished the likelihood that migrants would attempt to enter the United States, but has reduced cyclical migrants' inclination to return to Mexico, because the costs and risks associated with eventual re-entry to the United States are perceived by migrants to be too high. As a result, the post-IRCA era has been characterized by increased settlement and by the undocumented entry of more Mexican women joining spouses in the United States. In 1995, more than a quarter of undocumented migrants from Mexico were female (Cerrutti and Massey 2001). Undocumented migrants assume greater risks in the post-IRCA era by entering the United States at remote points subject to less vigilant patrols, or by traveling with smugglers under dangerous conditions. Finally, IRCA has led indirectly to the legal entry of the spouses, children, and other family members of newly legalized immigrants, dramatically increasing the number of foreign-born U.S. residents during the 1990's (Massey, Durand, and Malone 2002).

For parental households in Mexico, IRCA and the general focus of U.S. immigration on family reunification and skilled labor have had significant consequences for household organization because of the transition to more frequent migration by women, more frequent settlement, and because of increased undocumented entry by migrants who do not fit into the formal preference categories considered for legal entry. Increased migration by women implies that more daughters are abroad, either traveling alone or with spouses. The decision for daughters to migrate has significant consequences for parental households in terms of immediate, flexible income sources and the provision of non-remunerated labor to maintain the household. Under conditions of economic change, daughters are a flexible source of labor, employed as pieceworkers at home, as domestic or informal workers outside, or in the formal labor market in response to household need. The activities and responsibilities of working daughters are more narrowly circumscribed in the parental household compared to sons' (Gonzalez de la Rocha 1994), and daughters' earnings typically go entirely into the household coffers. At the same time, daughters contribute to the reproduction of labor by carrying out the work of household maintenance and cleaning and cooking for other household members. When daughters become migrants, parental households lose these important contributions, at least temporarily, but may gain more income through remittances.

The experience and consequences of migration will be different for parental households with female migrants to the extent that the social process that defines the initiation of migration and the migrant experience for women is distinct from that for men. Compared to men, female migrants are more likely to travel to the United States when a spouse or sibling has preceded them, and they are more likely than men to seek legal means of entry (Palloni, Massey, Ceballos, Espinosa and Spittel 2001). Both women who enter as labor migrants and who enter for family reunification have a high likelihood of finding employment (Donato 1993), and daughters are as likely as sons to become workers in the United States (Cerrutti and Massey 2001). But women who seek work enter different employment paths compared to men in terms of their social connections, the nature of the work they seek, and the social and economic consequences of their employment (Hondagneu-Sotelo 2001; Hondagneu-Sotelo 2003; Massey, Arango, Hugo, Kouaouci, Pellogrino, and Taylor 1994).

The increase in permanent settlement by migrant children also has potentially significant consequences for the organization of parental households. Mexican households are more nuclearized than elsewhere in Latin America; adult children typically establish their own households within a few years of marriage. Therefore, settlement abroad does not necessarily diminish the ultimate size of the parental household in Mexico, but settlement may accelerate the household's dispersion if the household becomes increasingly unviable as an economic unit. Alternatively, nonmigrant siblings may remain in the parental household longer than they would otherwise in order to maintain the household economically. Empirically, this is an open question, but researchers looking at urban households have come to opposite conclusions about the effect of migration on the parental household based on their interpretation of the role of migration in the household economy. On the one hand, migration (not necessarily settlement abroad) may be a creative strategy to extend the economic productivity of the parental household (Selby, Murphy, and Lorenzen 1990). On the other hand, another study written after Mexico's peso devaluation crisis of the early 1990's concluded that permanent settlement abroad was a reaction to a dysfunctional national economy, and would lead to the accelerated breakup of parental households (Gonzalez de la Rocha 2001). The distinction between the two arguments lies in the expectation that permanent settlement in the United States represents disengagement from the parental household, while temporary migration is a form of extended integration.

Increases in undocumented migration by children have implications for parental households because of the risks and costs associated with illegal border crossings, undocumented migrants' marginalized status in the United States, and the likelihood of an extended stay abroad in order to avoid multiple crossings over a series of trips. Migrants who enter the United States with a smuggler pay enormous fees and potentially put their health and safety in jeopardy, depending on how the smuggler crosses the border. These costs and risks may introduce a source of conflict if children's migration is a less desirable strategy for other household members, like parents, who are involved in deciding who will migrate and when. A border crossing made in the care of a smuggler also may burden other household members with additional costs upfront. Undocumented migrants' marginalized status once in the United States affects parental households to the extent that undocumented migrants will have less recourse than legal immigrants or citizens if they are shortchanged on pay, and they may have difficulty finding an inexpensive and efficient means of transferring remittances to the parental household without the identification required to open a bank account. Similarly, the costs of housing, health care, and transportation all may be inflated for migrants who lack the documents required to obtain a lease, health insurance, or car insurance. These costs of daily living will reduce migrants' savings and remittances. Finally, undocumented migrants' temporary stays may turn into *de facto* settlement over time if the risks and costs associated with entering and establishing oneself in the United States are too prohibitive to assume again.

RECENT DEVELOPMENTS IN MEXICO'S ECONOMY

Transitions in the Mexican economy during the last 20 years also draw attention to the significance of children's migration for parental households. Since 1982, Mexico has weathered financial crises that have weakened the ability of the state and the private sector to provide secure employment, health care, or pensions to most workers. The 1982 debt crisis emerged when revenues from Mexico's oil boom were insufficient to pay off the country's debts to international lenders. Wages plummeted and the percentage of families in poverty increased to 60 percent as a result. The centralized government turned to a policy of export-oriented industrialization financed by foreign investment that fundamentally transformed the nature of the Mexican economy and labor force. After 12 years under the new model, Mexico experienced a significant peso devaluation crisis in 1994, caused by mismanagement of the exchange rate and a weakening of the financial system supporting loans to Mexico's recently privatized banks. An unprecedented loan put together by the United States and the International Monetary Fund and a rapid increase of imports to the United States from Mexico temporarily buoyed Mexico's economy, but weaknesses at the macro level plagued the economy through the remainder of the decade.

The peso devaluation trailed on the heels of Mexico's entry into the North American Free Trade Agreement (NAFTA), which liberalized trade relations between Canada, the United States, and Mexico. NAFTA brought significant foreign investment to Mexico's assembly sector and greatly increased the volume of Mexico's exports to the United States. However, critics argue that dependence on the U.S. market for credit and exports and the faltering financial structure that supports export-led industrialization have led to greater income inequality, higher poverty levels, and higher unemployment (Bouillon, Loegovini, and Lustig 2003; Cypher 2001; Gonzalez de la Rocha 2001). As a result, families have increasingly used homework, the informal labor market, and international migration as strategies to maintain household economies. These sectors offer an alternative to labor force members who are unemployed in the formal sector, and also absorb workers not traditionally represented in the labor force, including married women with children.

Despite economic growth, Mexico still lacks a domestic investment strategy to provide universal access to education, health care, or economic security in old age. As a result, kin rely on one another for informal economic and instrumental support. Nationally in Mexico, women more than men among those over 65 rely on informal support, in part because their access to social security is more limited. The elderly receive help from coresidents (usually children) in the form of physical assistance, the provision of food, and other instrumental support. Non-resident kin (again, usually children) more often provide financial assistance. But the social networks of the elderly are relatively small, with most people relying on only one or two informal support providers (Montes de Oca 2001). A study restricted to Mexico City reported that men receive services and women receive money more often, mostly from coresident children. In turn, household heads over 60 frequently provide support to their coresident kin, with women providing services like child care, and men providing financial support (Palma 2001).

RESEARCH AGENDA

The preceding description of the history of Mexico-U.S. migration and parental households' social and economic circumstances in contemporary Mexico leads to the following research question: How do adult children, parents, and siblings in Mexico relate to each other in a culture of international migration? The aim of the remaining chapters is to address this question from the perspective of each of the actors considered.

First, the individual, household, and community-level factors that lead some children from the same family to migrate while others remain in Mexico are assessed. The analysis pays particular attention to the influences that differently affect sons and daughters, older and younger children, and rural and urban residents.

Second, the homeleaving decisions of nonmigrant children are considered. Are adult children more or less likely to live outside the parental household when they have siblings in the United States? Whether nonmigrant children delay or accelerate their own departure has significant consequences for the economic and social organization of the parental household, but there is little known about how and whether migrant and nonmigrant siblings interact in the interest of their common household.

Third, the economic benefits of children's migration to parents are considered. Do parents with children in the United States receive earnings transfers from children, and if so, from which children. The analysis considers various motives for children to transfer earnings to parents, and asks whether international migration makes a difference in the probability of receiving a transfer and the size of the transfer.

Before proceeding to the empirical research, the following two chapters provide the theoretical framework for the analysis and a description of the data sources.

CHAPTER 2

Models of Migration and Household Organization

Economists and sociologists have developed many theories to explain international migration processes based on the Mexico-U.S. experience. Micro-level theories explain the calculus an individual uses in making the decision to migrate, while structural approaches identify the macro conditions that propel select classes of people into migration streams. In between, theories that draw on the significance of social capital and cumulative migration experience highlight how family and community connections influence the initiation of migration and the quality of the migration experience. Empirical research indicates that the various theories complement one another to describe international migration as a predictable, definable process. The current review is restricted to theories of labor migration, which is the dominant mode of migration between Mexico and the United States.

NEOCLASSICAL MODELS

Neoclassical theories have been applied to models of migration behavior since the 1960s. Neoclassical models are characterized by assumptions common to traditional economic theory, including that the migrant is a rational actor operating with complete knowledge of his employment and earnings opportunities in the sending and receiving community. In the context of international migration, undocumented migrants are further able to calculate the risk of apprehension. With this information, workers perform a personal cost-benefit analysis, estimating future wages in the home community compared to wages in the potential receiving community, minus the costs and risks of getting there. If the latter is greater than the former, the worker migrates. Although neoclassical models are regarded in the sociological literature as incomplete, they continue to exert strong explanatory power in empirical tests of other migration theories (Massey et al. 1994).

Neoclassical economic models of labor migration (Lee 1966; Todaro 1969) treat migration as the outcome of a decisionmaking process between two players: the potential migrant and the labor market in the potential receiving country. These models describe labor migrants as atomized workers, divorced from the social and familial context that propels them into migration streams. Such contextual factors are *implicitly* incorporated into neoclassical models (Lee 1966), in that potential migrants are assumed to consider life cycle stages, access to information, and social capital in assessing the relative costs and benefits of traveling elsewhere for work (Pedraza-Bailey 1990). But the only observables in empirical tests of the neoclassical model are individual-level factors and attributes of the labor market in sending and receiving countries (Massey et al. 1994). Characteristics of the migrant's social and familial networks, as well as household characteristics like income and size, remain unexplored.

In neoclassical models, the worker is gender- and age-neutral, although the worker implicitly takes these factors into account when estimating potential earnings. For example, in neoclassical theory, human capital is an example of a compositional factor that explains how individuals assess wage disparities between origin and destination countries. Borjas (1999) explains the composition of Mexican migrants to the United States in terms of education and skill level. Migrants with less than a high school education typically occupy low-skill, low-wage occupations in the United States that pay better than comparable positions in Mexico. Better-educated Mexicans, in contrast, are not motivated to migrate because they are adequately remunerated in their own country. In Borjas's words, "As long as economic considerations matter in the migration decision, skills tend to flow to those markets that offer the highest value."

Although the migrant is motivated by the prospect of higher wages, his plans for those earnings are not incorporated into the traditional model. Specifically, models predicting migration do not indicate whether the wages are intended for individual consumption, investment, or support of children or other kin. Consequently, social roles apparently have no direct bearing on an individual's proclivity to migrate, or on how, or by whom, the decision to migrate is made. According to prior research based on neoclassical theory, Mexican migrants are motivated to travel to the United States for work because of wage disparities between the two countries. Despite decades of international migration, these wage disparities persisted through the twentieth century, with one of the largest per capita income gaps between neighboring countries in the world. In 2003, average GNP per capita in Mexico was about five times smaller than in the United States. Historically, the American economy has outpaced Mexico's, and increasingly, America's growth has relied in part on the contributions of migrant labor who satisfy demand in specific sectors for an inexpensive, dispensable work force that can be repatriated to the sending country during economic low points (Burawoy 1976; Piore 1979).

Responses to Neoclassical Models

Other microeconomic approaches have identified economic distortions in Mexico's local and national economy that affect individual landowners as causes of migration. Specifically, the new economics of migration (Stark and Taylor 1989) considers economic conditions within the migrant's sending community or country that additionally explain the motivation to migrate. Under this framework, the migrant is guided not only by the wage disparity between his country and the destination country, but by internal conditions as well. Inadequacies in internal conditions are often described as macro-level factors, like imperfect capital markets that discourage investment, a lack of credit that prevents entrepreneurship, high unemployment, and incomplete insurance markets. Some researchers have argued that in the last decade, macroeconomic conditions in Mexico have culminated in a crisis that has affected urban household organization and aggravated the demand for members to migrate for income (Cypher 2001; Gonzalez de la Rocha 2001).

Perceptions about local conditions also explain the motivation to migrate. Relative deprivation is one example of the information people use immediately around them to determine the need to migrate.

Relative deprivation is defined by Stark and Taylor (1989) as the perception that arises from intra-group inequalities where one person (or family or household) lacks and desires something that another person (family, household) in their social reference group possesses. In Mexico, the authors find that the greater a household's relative deprivation is, the higher is the probability of household members' labor migration, except at the lowest end of the income distribution, where families cannot afford the costs of migration.

The new economics of migration has been criticized by sociologists who focus on gender relations, because it considers only externally-imposed economic distortions, and consequently ignores the political economy of the household. Individual actors in households have competing perspectives on the costs and gains migration affords. Power differentials in the household that influence the migration outcome indicate that unequal access to power and resources exists within the household as well as outside (Pessar 2003).

STRUCTURAL APPROACHES

The neoclassical model has been criticized for failing to look outside the two-player model to see that macroeconomic forces operating in the world system lead to migration decisions that exacerbate economic inequality between countries, even as individuals strive to achieve economic equilibrium. As such, migration is both a symptom and a cause of increasing economic disparity (Wood 1982). Structuralists argue that migration decisions at the micro-level requires are contingent, in part, on the pre-existing macro conditions that propel select classes of people into migration streams.

Under a structural approach, the motives to migrate arise not from inequality at the individual level, but from inequalities that are produced between two countries or regions as a by-product of their economic relationship. In the country on the losing end of the relationship, options for employment, development, and enrichment are closed off in order to accommodate the wealthier country. In the case of the Mexico-U.S. relationship, production in agribusiness for export and the provision of relatively cheap labor in *maquiladoras* are two factors that push some individuals out of the national labor force and into migration streams. Two theories based on structural approaches use this perspective as a starting point to explain the case of Mexico-U.S. migration.

Segmented Labor-Market Theory

Segmented labor-market theory asserts that competitive capitalism in developed countries requires complementary spheres of production. One sphere employs a stable, skilled labor force to satisfy constant consumer demand. The other sphere, where migrants work, uses unskilled labor for temporary work during the high point of sector-specific economic cycles. Together, these spheres of production contribute to an efficient capitalist economy (Doeringer and Piore 1971).

Piore (1979) argues that migrants from poor countries are induced to come to rich countries by labor recruiters, who post new workers in sectors of the labor market that are no longer palatable to native-born workers. This arrangement is sanctioned both by employers and by unionized laborers in the receiving country, who are willing to host a temporary labor force that can absorb the downturn in economic cycles. Conflict arises only when migrants settle, or rather, fail to return to the sending country, and begin to compete for more desirable jobs.

The composition of labor migrant streams under this framework is pre-determined by recruiters from the receiving country. Employers require only that segment of the free labor market be willing and able to work in a circumscribed set of occupations. Laborers are targeted depending on their capacity to work in specific fields, typically in the agriculture, manufacturing, and service sectors. Depending on the content of the work, recruiters attract men or women, young workers or old. All workers who can satisfy the work requirements are eligible to migrate. The question then becomes, of the suitable potential laborers, who are the people who migrate internationally, and who stays in the sending community?

This question is hard to answer with a demand-based theory. In the dual labor-market framework, the migrant is initially passive, traveling to the receiving country only as long as he is sought after. The mechanisms that lead some qualified workers from within a family or community to travel to the receiving country while others stay behind are not clear. Although human capital characteristics are regarded as insufficient to explain selection, the framework lacks a conceptual model that explains the rest of the selection process.

Looking at migrants as household members offers a source of explanation that also considers economic context. Migrants are typically attached to a household where they occupy several social and familial roles, as son or daughter, husband or wife, and as caregiver, social conduit, or wage earner. Leaving the household as a migrant means that those social roles will be occupied by someone else or neglected. Whether one will migrate may be influenced as much by the individual's attributes and responsibilities to his household as by the capacity of others to assume his role. Alternatively, the decision depends on whether the household can adapt successfully without those role expectations being satisfied. But these considerations alone do not fully explain the decision at the household level to select one person as a migrant over another. Given the assumption that the objective of labor migration is to work and to earn money, the earnings potential and the willingness and capacity of individuals to contribute remittances or savings to others in the household will also influence judgment about who the most appropriate migrant would be.

Modes of Incorporation

Portes and Bach (1985) also develop a structural approach that criticizes the neoclassical economic model of migration behavior (also see Portes 1995). They argue that the neoclassical model ignores heterogeneity in the historical timing and class and ethnic composition of immigrant groups. The authors argue that these factors are more significant than are individual attributes in explaining modes of incorporation into the receiving country's society. They illustrate their argument with evidence from a longitudinal study of Cuban and Mexican immigrants legally admitted to the United States in 1973. The authors identify the ethnic enclave as a third sector of the capitalist economy that supplements the dual-labor market structure observed by Piore (1979).

Portes and Bach argue that Cuban immigrants to the United States succeeded in developing an ethnic enclave because of opportunities resulting from the intersection of historical timing and variation in the socioeconomic status of the pool of immigrants. The first wave of

Cubans to the United States to arrive during Castro's regime (post-1959) received a relatively hospitable political and economic welcome compared to Mexican migrants. Cuban immigrants who brought cash resources to the United States established small businesses and hired family members and less well-off workers in lower-status positions. The arrangement succeeded because business owners were able to couch demanding work requirements in terms of family obligation and ethnic cohesion. Workers cooperated because they expected to advance farther than they would in the non-enclave economy, and frequently these expectations were satisfied.

Contemporary Mexican migrants, by contrast, typically do not arrive in the United States with sufficient savings to launch a small enterprise. Most Mexicans arrive asset-poor and with only enough cash to subsist for a short time before finding work. Portes and Bach argue that the lack of distinct economic classes within and across waves of Mexican migrant groups explains why they have achieved less economic and occupational success in the United States.[5]

But class is not the only significant factor that explains the success of the Cuban enclave compared to Mexican migrants. Gender is another important component. Although most women from the Cuban middle- and upper-classes in the first wave of immigrants arrived in the United States with no work experience, their labor contributions (made without direct remuneration) helped to launch family enterprises in the receiving community. At the same time, Cuban women maintained the household or trained other family members to take over their responsibilities. By comparison, male Mexican migrants frequently travel without a spouse or children. An extension of Portes and Bach's theory would state that a flexible division of labor is required *within* immigrant households as well as *between* households in order to successfully adapt to new ways of working and earning. To test such a

---

[5] Political conditions at origin represent another important compositional factor in comparisons of Cuban and Mexican immigrants. Cuban immigrants arrived in the United States planning to remain until the Castro-led Communist regime in their origin country was overturned. If those immigrants anticipated a long stay, they might have been more willing to invest savings in the United States. Mexican migrants or immigrants, in contrast, have historically lacked a political disincentive to return to their origin country.

theory requires that we consider how households are organized in terms of work and living, in order to understand how and why social roles and responsibilities change for household members.

In sum, structural arguments take migration behavior beyond rationalistic individual decision-making. By identifying group-level characteristics of migrants and by theorizing about the underlying shape of the labor market, structuralists explain the functions of migrant labor in the American economy and give form to a process that was previously defined in atomistic terms. However, these macro approaches ignore the significance of the households as a fundamental organizing unit in society (Schmink 1984), and ignore how household members interact with the labor market and economy differently depending on factors like gender, education, and age.

Structural Approaches and the Case of Mexico-U.S. Migration

Mexico-U.S. labor migration in the aggregate supports structural approaches to migration theory. Segmented labor-market theory offers an explanation for why Mexican labor migrants historically have been young men obtaining seasonal employment. After the Mexican-American War concluded in 1848, Mexican men pursued labor opportunities offered by recruiters in mining, railroad construction, and agriculture (Gomez-Quinones 1994; Sanchez 1993). In later generations, men have found work in light manufacturing, construction, and services like restaurants, gardening, and maintenance. Unlike European immigrants in the late nineteenth and early twentieth centuries, Mexican migrants and their families have not typically saved up to settle in the United States, at least prior to the passage of IRCA in 1986. Rather, Mexican families have benefited from proximity to a relatively porous border and differences in the cost of living. Those factors, combined with seasonal employment, have enabled migrants to return to their families in the sending communities at least sporadically, if not regularly. When migrants return, the expectation is that they come with American dollars that will stretch farther than they would in the United States, where the costs of consumption and the reproduction of labor are higher. Whether this outcome is a choice migrants make, or the outcome of economic, political, and legal mechanisms to discourage settlement in the United States, is a question still under debate.

The documentation status of Mexican migrants is another important compositional factor that structural approaches address. Segmented labor market theory explains the initial placement of undocumented migrants in competitive, low-paying industries, while the modes of incorporation theory provides a framework to understand why undocumented migrants are unlikely to become integrated into the social structure of the receiving country over time, even if they settle there. As Piore (1979) showed, documentation status plays a critical role in determining a migrant's potential for pay, job stability, job advancement, and time in the receiving country. Undocumented workers typically occupy low-paying manual labor positions in industries that respond to economic downturns with swift layoffs. Documented workers, in contrast, find more secure positions with opportunities for advancement.

This distinction is partly a function of the freedom and mobility associated with legal status itself, and partly a result of to whom the United States grants legal entry. In the United States, one-third of visas allotted annually go to professional workers who are admitted to work in specific high-tech and/or high-skill sectors like computer programming and medicine.[6] Although there is demand in low-skill sectors for low-cost labor, the federal government currently has no broad program that would sanction the temporary entry and employment of migrant workers in such occupations.[7]

Few documented immigrants from Mexico arrive with work visas. The United States allows legal entry to skilled workers, as well as to Mexican tourists and family members of permanent residents and

---

[6] INS policy also allows entry of 10,000 preferential unskilled immigrants. Although INS policy is to grant one-third of visas based on work preference, that proportion may be smaller in the end if exemptions are made to allow other family-based entry, as was the case in 1996.

[7] The first administration of George W. Bush considered a temporary-worker program that would eventually grant permanent residence to some workers in agriculture and other manual labor occupations, but consideration was shelved after the World Trade Center and the Pentagon were attacked in 2001. A discussion between Mexico and the United States about new pathways to legal migration did not resume until November 2004.

citizens who have been granted visas. But in contrast to countries like India, China, and Russia, Mexico sends relatively few immigrants to occupy professional positions. Rather, the majority of legal entrants to the United States from Mexico travel under family reunification visas. In recent years, and especially after the passage of IRCA, married women have obtained visas to join Mexican husbands in the United States as laborers, keepers of the household, and companions (Donato 1993). The sudden increase in the size of the legal immigrant population after IRCA led to a commensurate rise in the number of requests for family reunification visas issued to spouses, parents, and children (Smith and Edmonston 1997).

Structural approaches suggest that men's seasonal labor migration from Mexico to the United States has been a particular response to capitalism's demand for a division of labor in both the public and private spheres. In the public sphere, the divisions have been multidimensional: at different times and in different sectors, gender, education, class, age, race, and nationality have all provided the basis for occupational stratification. In the current context, young men historically have been selected into migration streams for a number of reasons, including the demand for hard physical labor in occupations rejected by native workers; a desire by recruiters to keep workers sex-segregated in order to discourage family formation in the United States; and a history in Mexico in which women did not perform wage labor outside the home. In the private sphere in Mexico through most of the twentieth century, working-age men have not been involved in the renewal of labor at home.

But more recently, U.S.-Mexican labor migration has expanded to include women employed in domestic service, assembly, and light manufacturing. In these industries, employers favor female migrants over men because of the perception that women are better skilled, more subservient, and more willing to accept low pay than their male counterparts. Women use distinct pathways to obtain employment in female-dominated sectors, and the nature and setting of the work contribute to gender-specific experiences of migration (Hondagneu-Sotelo 2003). Women working in private households as cleaners or child care providers are relatively isolated and dependent, particularly if they live in the employers' home (Hondagneu-Sotelo 2001). Women working in Hispanic-owned businesses in ethnic enclaves have lower wages, less opportunity for advancement, and fewer benefits compared to women in other labor market sectors (Gilbertson 1995).

Social Capital and Cumulative Causation

A third perspective, social capital theory, stands between atomistic neoclassical models and broad macrostructural explanations. In relevant studies, social capital is regarded as the totality of potential or actual resources that "accrue to an individual or a group by virtue of possessing a durable network of more or less institutionalized relationships of mutual acquaintance and recognition (Bourdieu and Wacquant 1992; cited in Massey, Durand, and Malone 2002)." The network hypothesis, based on social capital theory, predicts that by drawing on one's social ties to migrants, an individual can minimize the risks and costs associated with initiating his own migration (Massey and Espinosa 1997). In the context of Mexico-U.S. migration, individuals with ties to migrants who can assist in crossing borders, obtaining documentation, and finding work and housing in the United States are more likely to become migrants than are those who lack such ties. These new migrants then become a rich source of social capital to potential migrants who know them.

Under social capital theory, the motivation to migrate is the product of two conditions: first, economic need, defined either in neoclassical or structural terms; and second, the availability of social capital that can be converted into access to migration streams. If a household experiences economic need but does not have any connections to facilitate the migration process, including border crossing and finding work and housing in the receiving country, household members may choose another option to satisfy need, including internal migration, entering more household members into the labor force, taking on second jobs, or selling assets. Conversely, if a household does not have any economic need (whether absolute or relative), its members may convert its social capital into access to other resources.

The pool of social capital resources available in a family or community changes as the composition of migration flows changes, becoming larger and more diverse in terms of social class, gender, and age. Over time, the costs and risks associated with migration decrease broadly as social networks overlap, access to the necessary social capital increases, and migration becomes institutionalized in a sending community. As a result of steadily growing access to social capital, migration processes become self-perpetuating, and operate apart from the logic of demand for labor, wage differentials, or other market-based incentives to migrate. This tendency in migrant-sending communities for migration to evolve into a feedback system is referred to as "cumulative causation (Massey et al. 1994)." Empirical evidence indicates that cumulative causation is a powerful explanation for the quality and quantity of Mexico-U.S. migration (Donato, Durand, and Massey 1992; Massey and Espinosa 1997), although it is less influential in urban compared to rural areas (Fussell and Massey 2004).

The magnitude of permanent and temporary migration from Mexico to the United States is unparalleled in recent migration history. For potential migrants, this means that there are ever more resources available for information and assistance in both countries. These resources can help to make entry to the United States, whether legal or illegal, safer, easier, and less expensive.

According to INS estimates, approximately 20 percent of all legal immigrants to the United States in 2000 were born in Mexico (Immigration and Naturalization Service 1997). In addition, an estimated 4.8 million undocumented migrants of Mexican origin lived in the United States in that year. If recent trends persist, this number will continue to rise steadily: between 300,000 and 400,000 migrants entered the United States illegally[8] each year during the 1990s (Immigration and Naturalization Service 2003). The magnitude of migration flows means that in some Mexican sending communities, the male labor force is essentially gutted during the migration season, leaving behind a community of children, women, and the elderly. In the Mixteca region of Oaxaca, for example, as many as 90 percent of men have accumulated migration experience (Guidi 1993).

However, emigration largely offsets the number of immigrants. Jasso and Rozenzweig (1990) find that as many as 40 percent of immigrants admitted as permanent resident aliens between 1970 and

---

[8] Illegal entry is defined as entering the United States without any documentation, overstaying a temporary visa, or working without authorization.

1979 left in that decade.[9] Among those from the western hemisphere, rates of return rose during the 1970's relative to the 1960's, suggesting an increasing tendency to return to one's country of origin after securing U.S. residency. Undocumented immigrants also emigrate at high rates: Based on a residual analysis employing Census data from 1980 and 1990, the INS estimates that approximately 80,000 undocumented Mexicans leave the United States annually (approximately 30 percent of all unauthorized inflows from Mexico) (Immigration and Naturalization Service 1997).[10] Massey and Singer (1995) estimate even higher emigration rates in some years, concluding that 86 percent of all undocumented entries between 1965 and 1990 were offset by departures.[11] This circularity offers new migrants security at both ends of their trip, and possibly facilitates the journey as well.

Two contributions from social capital theory help to focus the research questions stated in chapter 1. First, social capital theories predict that individuals are strongly influenced by the behavior of their fellow household and family members. Palloni and his co-authors (Palloni, Massey, Ceballos, Espinosa, and Spittel 2001) find that having a migrant sibling increases the likelihood of U.S. migration by three times when controls for human capital, unobserved heterogeneity, and common conditions are introduced.

---

[9] These data were the most recent available to the authors and included annual registration data on permanent resident aliens that was discontinued in 1980.

[10] The volume of emigration for migrants from all countries increased during the 1990's, but country-specific rates are not available (U.S. Immigration and Naturalization Service 2003).

[11] The difference in return migration rates calculated by the INS (1997) and by Massey and Singer (1995) is substantial. The two studies employ different data and methods to arrive at their conclusions. The INS study is based on the *absence* of immigrants from the later wave of Census data. The Massey and Singer analysis is based on reports of return migration by former migrants residing in Mexico and current migrants in the United States. The predicted rates of in-migration and out-migration are assumed to be representative of all of Mexico, although the survey was conducted in central and western Mexico only.

Second, social capital theories also recognize that different people have access to different types of social capital, which in turn grant access to distinct ends. Gender is an obvious example as it relates to Mexico-U.S. migration. In Mexico, men and women typically operate in separate spheres in day-to-day life. The crudest distinction would be that women maintain the private sphere while men negotiate the public sphere. But even when women enter the public sphere to work, they typically join sex-segregated occupations, both in the formal and informal labor force.

The feedback system that evolves among male migrants under these conditions is likely to be male-dominated. Without sex-integrated social institutions within Mexico where social capital may be exchanged, women are unlikely to gain access to the dominant migration system. Consequently, women are required to find other avenues to migration, including marriage, accompanying a close male relative from within the household, or gaining entry to social networks occupied by women with migration experience.

Taking these contributions from social capital theory together, we can ask how children from a common household of origin differ in their access to the social capital that inheres within that household. Does access to forms of social capital vary among individuals all the way down to the household, both in terms of the quantity of social capital, and the type? And how, and by whom, is that social capital repaid to the household?

Summary of the Migration Literature

The preceding review of the migration literature summarized theories about why and how people migrate, particularly for work. Some reasons people migrate include a quest for better pay, either to satisfy absolute or relative need; a response to demand for labor from employers abroad; and the increasing ease of migration as the process becomes institutionalized in sending communities.

The theories described also help to explain why Mexico-U.S. labor migration has been characterized historically by the cyclical movement of young men frequently traveling without documentation. Explanations include the relatively good remuneration for unskilled male labor, compared to that for unskilled women and skilled men in

Mexico; the feasibility of split-household strategies across borders resulting from a division of labor in the sending household; the demand for cheap labor in sectors where employers are willing to take the risks associated with hiring undocumented workers; and the nature of social networks that enable some people to migrate more readily than others. Although these theories explain a great deal of the variation in migration processes, they do not describe the context in which migration decisions are made, or where the consequences of those decisions are felt. The following section describes the parental household as such a context. Using a household framework introduces a setting where social roles as kin and migrant intersect.

MODELS OF HOUSEHOLD FUNCTIONING

Studies of household behavior bridge the gap between social and individual levels of analysis (Schmink 1984; Wood 1982). As one of the most basic economic units in society, the household creates and constrains individual responses to structural conditions, and thus circumscribes the scope of behaviors open to individuals as producers and consumers. In the context of international migration, this means that household members respond to the decline of local economic opportunities or the rise in opportunities elsewhere by selecting some members to move away from home for work (Wood 1982).

Research in sociology and economics provides various models to understand how the household operates. Three of those models have been applied to scholarship on migration. They are known respectively as *the household as moral economy, the household strategies model,* and *the household bargaining approach.* Each makes different assumptions about how households respond to change, and how household decisions are made. While research derived from each framework has made useful contributions to what we know about migration, the last is the most widely used.

The Household as Moral Economy

In the household as moral economy approach, collective interests are put above individual interests. When the household is considered as a strategic unit, the emphasis is on jointly maximizing income and minimizing economic risk. Both models are characterized by the assumption that the household is a cohesive, functional unit where individuals suppress their own preferences so that everyone may adapt equally well to changing external conditions. Differences in relative power and in access to resources among household members either are assumed not to exist or to be a moot point because everyone is acting in the common interest (Folbre 1986).

In the moral economy model, the household is conceived as an economic unit whose members are bound by a social and moral imperative to assist one another. One application is the New Home Economics model, which asserts that within the household, certain responsibilities, or spheres of production, are assigned to different members of the unit in ways that make the most economic sense (Becker 1991). Household members act on common interests and pool resources in order to maximize their joint utility function. This model has been applied to empirical tests of theories about the gendered division of labor in the household, most often as it relates to husbands and wives. The underlying assumption is that each member is doing the task to which he or she is best suited in order to achieve the shared goal of a maximally productive household.

A resulting theoretical model of migration and remittances assumes that the household is altruistic and that members operate under a "self-enforcing, cooperative, contractual agreement (Stark and Taylor 1989, p. 465)" in which different actors (migrants and nonmigrants) accrue benefits from migration at different points in time. Although self-interest and bargaining power figure into the contract, these non-altruistic traits neatly come out in the wash over time. In an empirical illustration, rural-urban migrants in Botswana get more education than do nonmigrant siblings in order to raise their human capital and earn higher wages; the migrant is expected to repay the family for that investment through remittances or savings; the migrant's wages are received as a form of insurance, thus allowing the family to assume greater risks in agriculture; and the migrant continues to remit in the hope of eventually inheriting more land than his siblings (Lucas and Stark 1985; Stark and Lucas 1988).

In this example, individual self-interests are traded over time, with the expectation that everyone will eventually be satisfied. The model assumes that although various interests dominate at different points in time, those interests are static. That is, a migrant who begins his urban career hoping to inherit the family land will maintain that ambition throughout his working life, and families will continue to use remittances to invest in agriculture, rather than in education, business, or consumption. In sum, this aspect of the model does not allow for the emergence of new interests in response to changing conditions internal or external to the household.

Burawoy (1976) argues that states exploit the discrete division of labor in the "moral economy" household by underpaying migrant workers with the expectation that the renewal of wage labor will be carried out in the sending country by household members not in the labor force. In fact, other empirical work indicates that migration from Mexico is male-dominated partially as a consequence of women's domestic obligations (Selby, Murphy, and Lorenzen 1990).

However, women's obligations are not restricted to the domestic sphere. Rather, women work as informal laborers[12] before and during the migration of husbands, sons, and brothers in order to raise money for the trip and to sustain over the short-term those members who remain (Dinerman 1978; Kanaiaupuni and Fomby 2000). This transition from the private to the public sphere arises from the household head's devaluation of the opportunity costs associated with the work women do outside of the household to compensate for another worker's absence (Dinerman 1978).

Household Strategies Model

These findings lend support to the *household strategies model*, which asserts that households actively respond to changes in external economic conditions by re-allocating labor and material resources to achieve specific goals. The number of consumers and producers in the household and group-level access to income constrain the household's ability to strategize. This model expands on Becker's New Home Economics model, derived from the moral economy framework, by

---

[12] Entrepreneurs and their employees providing goods and services outside of the institutionalized structures of the economy. This category includes street vendors, itinerant workers, and families selling food and other goods from their homes. The labor and/or commodity exchange is generally characterized by cash transactions and evasion of the federal, state, and local tax systems.

making the household active and dynamic. That is, members may alter their roles in order to adapt to changing conditions.

Wood (1981) provides an example of the place of migration within a household strategies framework. Migration is treated as one adaptive strategy that the household pursues in response to changing structural conditions like the transition to a capitalist mode of production. However, migration is not selected as a strategy in a vacuum; rather, migration is conditional on "the success or failure of other initiatives undertaken to maintain (or increase) the level of consumption and reproduction(1981, p. 341)." Unlike the neoclassical models described earlier where migration is the outcome of isolated negotiations between the worker and the market, or in the altruistic model where the objectives of migration are static, the household strategies model stresses that migration behavior is a dynamic component of interrelated processes across the household.

An example from rural households in the highlands of southern Peru highlights the dynamic relationship between external conditions and individual roles and responsibilities inside the household (Collins 1985). Because of governmental, environmental, and economic disincentives to produce food for sale locally, farming households select various members for wage labor migration and off-site coffee production. This response to external changes leads to an internal re-ordering of responsibilities, including women's participation in managing family-owned land, the increased productivity of young children, and disengagement from kin and community networks that organize the subsistence community.

Several studies conducted in Mexico during the 1980's used a household strategies approach to understand economic organization in urban households, but did not focus on the role of migration. They found that for working class household heads in urban areas, the only way to improve economic standing is through the household. Over the course of a career, workers do not systematically receive wage increases, so quality of life does not necessarily improve with job tenure, assuming that a worker even remains with the same employer over a working lifetime. Instead, the better-off households are those that have more children of working age, more workers, a lower dependency ratio, and more migration (Selby, Murphy, and Lorenzen 1990). Economic crises like those experienced in Mexico in the early 1980's and early 1990's exacerbate the need for more workers per household in response to men's unemployment and underemployment (Gonzalez de la Rocha 1994). In rural areas as well, parents have an incentive to retain children as workers in the household: parental households with *ejido* landholdings use children's labor in order to maximize their comparative advantage of lower labor costs compared to private agriculture (deJanvry, Gordillo, and Sadoulet 1997). As a result, the heads of better-off households in both urban and rural areas are reluctant to lose household members to new family formation. In later work, Gonzalez de la Rocha (2001) argued that Mexico's eroding employment opportunities during the 1990's were overwhelming the potential for poor households to survive by pooling incomes, and predicted a crisis of social reproduction for the urban working class.

Despite the advantages of the household strategies framework relative to the moral economy framework, the household strategies approach makes two falsifiable assumptions, as later research indicates: first, that household members have equal access to household resources, and are equally invested in preserving the household unit; and second, that all household members agree on strategies and on the ends they seek to achieve. In addition, the variables that affect strategic capacity in these models are economic in nature, and ignore important norms, traditions, and expectations about gender roles and kinship (Grasmuck and Pessar 1991).

Arizpe's (1982) comparison of traditional peasant economies in transition in Mexico provides a relevant example of these assumptions. In order to supplement local earnings, household members rotate in and out of migration streams according to age, position in the household, and the household's stage in the domestic life cycle. Where the household economy is relatively stable, the shared goal is to save remittances for the future; in communities where local opportunities have deteriorated, migration is a continuous process intended to satisfy immediate need. In either situation, the goal of household survival, and the means to achieve it, are assumed to be shared by migrants and nonmigrants alike.

Household Bargaining Model

More recent research conducted from a gendered perspective argues that the division of labor in the household is neither so rational, so altruistic, nor so maximizing as these examples suggest. Rather, household members have competing interests that change over time, and one's ability to satisfy those interests is a function of relative power in the household (Folbre 1986; Grasmuck and Pessar 1991; Hondagneu-Sotelo 2003; Katz 1991).

This approach, drawn from the economics literature on *household bargaining* (Nash 1950), is characterized by a model that describes households living in "cooperative conflict (Sen 1990)." The model has been applied primarily to decisionmaking processes between spouses that influence outcomes relating to labor force participation, health and nutrition, and household expenditures (Oppenheimer 1994; Thomas 1991).

The household bargaining model is also well-suited conceptually to research on the decisionmaking processes that precede international migration. Migration is an economic strategy with unique risks and opportunities: the economic benefits are slow to arrive, if they do at all, and undocumented migrants face the costly and dangerous risk of becoming ill on the journey or being apprehended by border guards or swindled by smugglers. Although most migrants ultimately earn higher wages in the destination area than they would at home, there is no guarantee of success in finding work. Even after securing employment, the migrant still has to support himself, safely remit his earnings to the family waiting at the other end, and avert illness, accidents, and crime in order to make his trip profitable.

Given these risks, migrants and nonmigrants might have different views about whether migration is in fact a sensible strategy. A nonmigrant might prefer the safety and security of the potential migrant's presence, fearing that his or her absence will lead to greater hardships than would the status quo for the family members who remain. Even former migrants may fear for the well-being of siblings or children who travel abroad (see Gonzalez-Lopez 2004). A potential migrant, on the other hand, might operate with greater information or with false hopes about job prospects, giving him or her a different view of the journey. Each will employ a distinct decisionmaking calculus as well. While nonmigrants might focus on economic benefits and threats to safety, migrants might take into account the social component of migration, considering the trip as a rite of passage in the sending community, or as an obligation to a friend or family member. Each household member will consider different aspects of migration, and weigh those components differently in order to determine the merit of an international trip. When these estimations are in conflict, the final decision about whether to migrate becomes a function of power relations in the household.

The bargaining approach has been useful for problematizing the household and bringing the competing interests of household members into relief. For example, in the Dominican Republic of the early 1960's, husbands and wives and fathers and sons had different views of the value of using migration as a safety valve for surplus family labor during the transition from subsistence farming to capitalist agriculture staffed by hired laborers. Fathers initially encouraged their oldest sons to travel to New York in order to free up the family landholding for cash crops, but sons wanted to inherit the land in order to begin to establish independent households. However, these views changed over time. Fathers eventually decided that this arrangement was not profitable and discouraged younger sons from migrating, but, after being exposed to U.S. migrant culture, these children were intent on traveling to the United States to explore more diverse opportunities. Wives also became interested in traveling to New York, where they could work for wages without being stigmatized as they were in the Dominican Republic (Grasmuck and Pessar 1991).

In other contexts, different patterns of selecting migrants arise. For example, in Thai households with at least three adult children, the middle child is most likely among his siblings to migrate seasonally, and middle daughters are most likely to remit wages. In contrast, older children, particularly sons, are expected to pursue an education or work in the local community, and younger children are expected to care for the parents in the household (Curran 1996). From focus group discussions, Curran reports that Thai respondents indicate that the middle child cannot be "depended on" like the others and usually elects to migrate, and that social roles are more clearly defined for older and younger children. Quantitative analyses support this description of behavior patterns within families.

In the Mexican-U.S. context, much has been written about power relations between husbands and wives, and how migration influences gender relations to change the balance of power. In the United States, married migrant women report feeling more personal autonomy and independence, greater equity with their husbands in the division of household labor and more emotional intimacy, and greater access to the social and economic resources available in the public sphere (Hirsch

2003; Hondagneu-Sotelo 1994; Pedraza 1991; Pessar 2003). However, less is known about how power relations between parents and children influence the selection of children to migrate, or how relations between generations change in response to children's migration.

Children who become migrants may do so as a response to demands from one or both parents, or may decide independently or in conjunction with a sibling, friend, or spouse to migrate. In the case of parental control, the decision may be made by the head alone: in the stereotypical Mexican family, authority rests ultimately with the head, and other family members cooperate with his demands or rebel on the margins. But Mexican households in reality are more complex than the stereotype implies. Women's power and autonomy in the household have increased in response to gains in women's education and labor force participation and role changes that have accompanied household-level responses to economic crises (Casique 2001). As a result, spouses may decide jointly whether their own migration or their children's migration is economically beneficial to the household. But children also look to their peers to weigh the migration decision. Siblings motivate one another, so that the migration history of an older sibling is potentially a more significant factor even than a parent's migration background in the choice to migrate (Palloni et al. 2001). And in communities with a long tradition of U.S.-bound migration, children anticipate migration as a rite of passage (Kandel and Massey 2002), and parents' opinions may be less influential than those of peers and returned migrants.

The preceding review of the literatures on international migration and household structure points to a complex set of conditions that adult children who become migrants must navigate. The choice to become a migrant and the subsequent experience are influenced by power relations and role responsibilities in the parental household, by the availability of social capital and social support from other relatives and community, and by the political and economic climate in both the sending and receiving countries. Children's migration in turn influences the institutions involved in the process through the contributions of remittances to families, influences on civic organization in sending and receiving communities, and direct and indirect effects on local labor markets. The analysis in the forthcoming chapters focuses on how adult children who become migrants fit into their parental households, but the social and economic climate provides a necessary backdrop.

The analysis addresses three questions. First, in the context of the parental household, who becomes a migrant? The research focuses on how common background characteristics interact with the attributes of individual household members to produce distinct chances of migration. These interactions are potentially important not only for uncovering variation within the household in migration probabilities, but also for contributing to a life course perspective on how migration serves the household over time. Exploration of these interactions is intended to explain changes in the purpose of migration and consequent differences in the role of migrant children in the parental household. As the Thai context suggests, some children migrate as potential earners for their families, while others migrate because they have the fewest ties to or responsibilities in the household. In that case, an adult child's social roles carry over to how the child relates to the household of origin as a migrant after departure.

The second question considers the extent to which children's migration influences the organization of the parental household. Generally speaking, migration trends alter general patterns of household composition and social roles in Mexican families. Adult daughters traditionally remain in their parents' home until marriage, and adult sons remain in the home with their wives until they can afford to establish an independent household (Sanchez 1993). Although families in Mexico are less likely to live in extended households than are families elsewhere in Latin America (DeVos 1995), adult children in Mexican households leave home later than American children, who are increasingly likely to separate home-leaving and marriage into distinct life course stages (see Goldscheider and Goldscheider 1993).

Migration leads to an earlier break from the household of origin by coupling labor-force entry and home-leaving for young Mexican men and women who travel to the United States in search of work. Therefore, children's migration influences living arrangements in the parental household, both directly through the absence of those children, and potentially through the choices nonmigrant siblings make about the timing of their own home-leaving. Nonmigrants may accelerate their departure in what Gonzalez de la Rocha (1994) has characterized as a process of dispersion. Alternatively, they may remain in the parental household, perhaps to serve their own interests by delaying the cost of establishing a separate household, or in a unified effort to make the parental household a more economically productive unit.

The third question considers migrants as participants with parents, siblings, and kin in an ongoing exchange of resources. Specifically, the research considers whether parents with children in the United States receive earnings transfers from children, and if so, from which children. The analysis considers various motives for children to transfer earnings to parents, and asks whether international migration makes a difference in the probability of receiving a transfer and the size of the transfer.

CHAPTER 3

The Shape and Form of Parental Households in Mexico
A Descriptive Summary

This research employs survey data to evaluate the research questions posed at the end of chapter 1. The current chapter describes the survey data, and then provides a summary of the parental households represented by the data. The summary includes information on where in Mexico the households are, who resides there, the economic and social resources available to the household and the community, and the past and current migration experiences of parents and children. This description is useful for getting a familiarity with Mexican households before proceeding to multivariate analyses that focus on specific attributes of the household and its members in order to assess the role of children's migration.

DATA

Data for this research come from two sources: The Mexican Migration Project (MMP, 2003), managed jointly at the University of Pennsylvania and the University of Guadalajara, and the Health and Migration Survey (HMS, 2003), managed at Rice University.

The Mexican Migration Project

The MMP is an ethnosurvey[13] administered in Mexican communities and in destination areas in the United States since 1982. The data used in the current research were collected in about 15,000 households in 93 communities in western and central Mexico between 1987 and 2002. The MMP has several strengths that make it suitable for considering the research questions posed here. First, extensive information about the migration experience in the household is available. The ethnosurvey obtains information from the household head about his own migration history and that of his spouse[14,15] within Mexico and in the United States. Data include the year that each trip began and ended, the migrant's occupations during each trip, and, for trips to the United States, the migrant's legal status and the nature of his border crossings. Comparable data about timing, duration, occupation, and legal status are collected for the adult children of the household head, but pertain only to their first and most recent trips within Mexico or to the United States. These data on adult children are fundamental to the analyses in the following chapters.

Second, the data include detailed demographic information collected from a household/family roster. Interviewers use the roster to gather information about age, sex, education, marital status, occupation,

---

[13] Massey and Zenteno Immigration and Naturalization Service. 2003. "Estimates of the Unauthorized Immigrant Population Residing in the United States: 1990 to 2000." Office of Policy and Planning, U.S. Immigration and Naturalization Service, Washington, DC. describe the ethnosurvey as "a multimethod data-gathering technique that simultaneously applies ethnographic and survey methods within a single study. The guiding philosophy is that qualitative and quantitative procedures complement one another and that, properly combined, one's weaknesses are the other's strengths, yielding a body of data with greater reliability and more internal validity than could be achieved using either method alone(2000, p.76) ."

[14] The household head is male in about 95 percent of cases.

[15] A full migration and work history has been collected for the spouse of male household heads since 1994. Previously, only data on the spouse's first and most recent migration within Mexico and to the United States were collected.

and relation to the household head for everyone living in the household at the time of interview, as well as for all of the head's children who are no longer living in the household.[16] These data enable hypothesis tests regarding the interaction of individual characteristics like age, sex, and birth order with other household attributes like migration history.

Third, the instrument collects information about the household's socioeconomic status over time. Specifically, data include the history of the household head's assets, such as land and property, as well as the characteristics of his primary dwelling. These data permit an assessment of the household's socioeconomic well-being prior to the predicted migration-related events.

MMP data are collected in communities in central and western Mexico[17] that represent a range of sizes and economic activities. Communities include towns with an economic base in agriculture, industry, or mining; larger metropolitan areas; and agrarian communities with varying patterns of land distribution and farming methods. Although the surveyed communities are not broadly representative of Mexico,[18] the sample does include variation in community type, with industries and economies that are common within Mexico at least partially represented (Massey, Goldring, and Durand 1994; Massey and Zenteno 2000).

Although the MMP focuses on western and central Mexico because of its historical significance in the volume of Mexico-U.S. migration flows, the sampled communities were not selected for migration prevalence. The percentage of adult residents in a community with migration experience ranges from 10 percent to 60 percent. As a result, "the database...embraces a diverse range of migratory experiences and is not composed exclusively of communities with well-developed migration streams (Massey and Zenteno 2000, p. 773)."

---

[16] A household membership variable indicates whether the children coreside with the household head.

[17] The majority of communities surveyed lie in five states: Guanajuato, Jalisco, Michoacán, San Luis Potosí, and Zacatecas.

[18] For example, Mexico's northern border region is more dependent on *maquiladoras* and agribusiness as sources of employment and economic stimulation than are the surveyed communities.

Between 100 and 200 households from each community are selected for interviewing using simple random sampling. Sampling frames are drawn by fieldworkers who conduct a door-to-door enumeration of households in each community. Table 3.1 shows the population size in each community, the year in which the survey was conducted, the final sample size, and the refusal rate. Refusal rates are relatively low, compared to American standards, with the exception of several urban communities interviewed in 2001.

The MMP database also includes data from interviews conducted in the United States in households that have permanently settled in selected communities. The respondents in the United States come from Mexican towns sampled during the preceding wave of data collection, and are found using snowball sampling techniques, beginning with information provided by respondents in Mexico. The U.S. sample is included to eliminate bias in the survey data that would result from interviewing only those households with no migration experience or with return migration experience. Households that have relocated to the United States are assumed to be different from those still in Mexico, and to have had a different experience with migration. Providing these binational data gives a more complete picture of how migration operates and affects communities of origin in Mexico.

Data collected in U.S. households are not presented here, because the analysis focus on the impact of migration on parental households that remain in Mexico. If the response to children's migration in some parental households is to pick up and follow, the results presented in my analyses will be biased to the extent that those migrating parental households are different from other households in Mexico. Including only households in Mexico makes the assumption that almost all parents stay behind when their children migrate to, and even settle in, the United States.

Table 3.1 Sample information summary from MMP93 communities

No.	State	1990 Pop.	2000 Pop.	Survey Year	Sample Size	Refusal Rate
1	Guanajuato	52,000	65,000	1987	200	0.034
2	Guanajuato	868,000	1,135,000	1987	200	0.119
3	Jalisco	4,000	5,000	1988	200	0.14
4	Guanajuato	17,000	18,000	1988	200	0.057
5	Guanajuato	2,000	2,000	1988	150	0.085
6	Jalisco	5,000	6,000	1988	200	0.115
7	Jalisco	3,000	4,000	1988	200	0.01
8	Michoacan	6,000	8,000	1989	200	0.05
9	Michoacan	32,000	36,000	1989	200	0.037
10	Michoacan	2,000	1,000	1990	150	0.152
11	Nayarit	20,000	25,000	1990	200	0.029
12	Nayarit	12,000	13,000	1990	200	0.01
13	Guanajuato	21,000	25,000	1990	200	0.047
14	Michoacan	7,000	8,000	1990	200	0.057
15	Guanajuato	265,000	319,000	1991	200	0.057
16	Guanajuato	1,000	1,000	1991	100	0.029
17	Jalisco	31,000	35,000	1991	200	0.044
18	Zacatecas	8,000	7,000	1991	365	0.127

Table 3.1 Sample Information Summary of MMP Communities, continued

No.	State	1990 Pop.	2000 Pop.	Survey Year	Sample Size	Refusal Rate
19	Michoacan	428,000	550,000	1991	200	0.083
20	Jalisco	3,000	3,000	1982	106	0.038
21	Jalisco	2,000	2,000	1982	94	0.037
22	Michoacan	7,000	7,000	1982	200	0.015
23	Jalisco	12,000	18,000	1982	200	0.038
24	Jalisco	1,650,000	1,646,000	1982	200	0.048
25	Jalisco	1,000	1,000	1992	100	0.029
26	Guanajuato	34,000	34,000	1992	200	0.095
27	Guanajuato	24,000	22,000	1992	200	0.127
28	Jalisco	73,000	85,000	1992	200	0.074
29	Michoacan	188,000	226,000	1992	200	0.083
30	Zacatecas	1,000	1,000	1991	187	0.025
31	Guerrero	83,000	105,000	1993	100	0.089
32	San Luis Potosi	489,000	629,000	200	25	0.048
33	Colima	7,000	8,000	1994	200	0.087
34	Zacatecas	2,000	2,000	1994	149	0.063
35	Zacatecas	100,000	114,000	1994	239	0.142
36	San Luis Potosi	13,000	13,000	1994	201	0.024

42

Table 3.1 Sample Information Summary of MMP Communities, continued

No.	State	1990 Pop.	2000 Pop.	Survey Year	Sample Size	Refusal Rate
37	San Luis Potosi	1,000	1,000	1994	102	0
38	San Luis Potosi	42,000	47,000	1994	200	0.052
39	San Luis Potosi	1,000	1,000	1994	100	0
40	Zacatecas	34,000	38,000	1995	201	0.107
41	Guerrero	7,000	6,000	1995	153	0.186
42	Guerrero	1,000	1,000	1995	100	0.107
43	Guerrero	515,000	621,000	1995	200	0.074
44	San Luis Potosi	1,000	1,000	1995	99	0
45	San Luis Potosi	1,000	1,000	1996	142	0
46	Zacatecas	1,000	1,000	1995	111	0.142
47	San Luis Potosi	3,000	4,000	1996	197	0.032
48	San Luis Potosi	3,000	4,000	1996	94	0.021
49	Oaxaca	1,000	1,000	1996	100	0
50	Oaxaca	1,000	1,000	1996	100	0
51	Oaxaca	9,000	9,000	1997	199	0.083
52	Oaxaca	213,000	252,000	1996	200	0.087
53	Sinaloa	2,000	1,000	1998	100	0.02
54	Puebla	1,007,000	1,272,000	1997	201	0.016
55	Guanajuato	1,000	1,000	1997	80	0

Table 3.1 Sample Information Summary of MMP Communities, continued

No.	State	1990 Pop.	2000 Pop.	Survey Year	Sample Size	Refusal Rate
56	Guanajuato	1,000	1,000	1998	87	0.033
57	Jalisco	4,000	6,000	1998	201	0.057
58	Jalisco	1,000	1,000	1998	100	0.029
59	Puebla	2,000	2,000	1997	100	0.01
60	Puebla	2,000	3,000	1997	100	0.01
61	Puebla	9999	9999	1998	199	0.05
62	Sinaloa	3,000	4,000	1998	150	0.02
63	Baja California Norte	699,000	1,149,000	1998	150	0.068
64	Baja California Norte	699,000	1,149,000	1998	150	0.011
65	Baja California Norte	699,000	1,149,000	1998	150	0.085
66	Baja California Norte	699,000	1,149,000	1998	152	0.08
67	Colima	3,000	4,000	1998	72	0.029
68	Colima	1,000	1,000	1998	100	0
69	Aguascalientes	18,000	4,000	1998	150	0.013
70	Sinaloa	5,000	6,000	1998	202	0.01
71	Aguascalientes	2,000	2,000	1997	100	0.01
72	Guanajuato	41,000	41,000	2000	155	0.094
73	Durango	16,000	23,000	1999	203	0.024
74	Durango	9,000	9,000	1999	151	0

Table 3.1 Sample Information Summary of MMP Communities, continued

No.	State	1990 Pop.	2000 Pop.	Survey Year	Sample Size	Refusal Rate
75	Durango	1,000	1,000	1999	101	0
76	Durango	348,000	427,000	1999	200	0
77	Nuevo Leon	-	226,000	2000	0	0.024
78	Chihuahua	4,000	5,000	2000	200	0.02
79	Chihuahua	3,000	4,000	2000	150	0
80	Chihuahua	516,000	516,000	2000	201	0.047
81	Chihuahua	1,000	1,000	2000	100	0
82	Chihuahua	789,522	1,189,275	2001	150	0.272
83	Chihuahua	789,522	1,189,275	2001	150	0.531
84	Chihuahua	789,522	1,189,275	2001	150	0.571
85	Chihuahua	789,522	1,189,275	2001	150	0.464
86	Nuevo Leon	4,699	5,057	2001	10	0
87	Guanajuato	758,279	1,020,818	2001	201	0.052
88	Guanajuato	37,845	45,691	2001	170	0.056
89	Guanajuato	10,381	12,558	2001	199	0.01
90	San Luis Potosi	581	924	2002	100	0.048
91	Jalisco	1,650,042	1,646,183	2002	200	0.429
92	Hidalgo	838	1,502	2002	105	0
93	Hidalgo	65,934	30,831	2002	201	0.199

Generalizability of the MMP Sample

A study comparing the MMP to a nationally representative household demographic survey[19] in Mexico shows that the MMP sample is similar on most dimensions (Massey and Zenteno 2000). Differences between the two samples result from intended differences in sample design. Those differences are important, however. First, compared to the nationally representative study, the MMP overstates the frequency of labor migration consistently across surveyed states. On average, the proportion of people over 12 years old in western Mexico who have labor migration experience is two percent higher in the MMP than in the Encuesta Nacional de la Dinámica Demográfica (ENADID). Furthermore, migrants from mid-sized communities in the area are overrepresented in the MMP, while migrants from rural areas and large metropolitan areas are underrepresented.

Another discrepancy between the MMP and the ENADID is also important. According to the MMP, about 27 percent of current or returned labor migrants are counted as sons or daughters to the household head. In contrast, only about 17 percent of current or returned migrants are counted as sons or daughters in the ENADID. The authors of the comparison study argue that this difference shows a strength of the MMP design: while the ENADID does not systematically inquire about the migration history of the head's children who are not "normally" residents of his household, the MMP asks about the migration history of all children, regardless of where they are currently living. As a result, the MMP captures data on children who are not considered current household residents because they are in the United States. The ENADID, in contrast, overlooks those migrants if they are not considered household members in Mexico.

Limitations to the MMP Data

Although the MMP data are well-suited to this research, there are some important limitations. First, some data are available only for the time of

---

[19] The ENADID survey (National Survey of Demographic Dynamics) was fielded in 1992.

interview. These data include the marital status and household membership of the head's adult children. Because we do not know the date when children married, or when they left or returned to the parental household, it is difficult to establish a *causal* relationship between migration and household change. This is a limitation particularly salient to the analyses in chapters 4 and 5.

The Health and Migration Survey

The Health and Migration Survey is a longitudinal study of the relationship between family health and international migration in Mexico and the United States. A pilot study was conducted in 1995 in eight communities in San Luis Potosí, Mexico, and an extensive follow-up interview was conducted in the same households between January and March 1996. In 1998, selected communities were re-interviewed, and new communities were added to the sample. The 1996 sample, which is used here, include approximately 1100 households.[20]

Households in four of the sampled communities were initially selected by the principal investigators in conjunction with the Mexican Migration Project in 1994. In the other four communities, interviewers affiliated with the Health and Migration Survey administered the MMP survey as part of the household interview.

Again, the sample was derived with simple random sampling methods and used a complete enumeration of the community as a sampling frame. Like the communities sampled in the MMP, those in the HMS represent a range of sizes, economic activities, and migration histories. Refusal rates for the 1996 sample are comparable to refusal rates in the MMP; they are relatively low by American standards, not exceeding 10 percent.

In contrast to the MMP, the survey respondent for the HMS is always female, whether she is the household head or the spouse of the

---

[20] A comparable survey was fielded in Houston, Texas and San Diego, California in the summers of 1996 and 1997. Approximately 250 households are included in that sample. The binational approach enables researchers to study health status and household organization before and after migration, as well as to study the transnational relationships migrants maintain with their sending communities. These data are not used in the current research.

head. Because one of the focal points of the study is health, much of the survey is devoted to collecting detailed information about the recent health of the woman, her husband, and her two youngest children under age 6; birth histories for all children under 6; the woman's knowledge about a range of health-related issues, including contraception, causes of illness, and the availability of health services in her community; and the woman's fertility history. The study also seeks to characterize women's experience of international migration and to understand household responses to migration events. Consequently, information is gathered about the respondent's social networks and migration and labor force experience, as well as the organization of the household economy, including sources of income, expenditures, and control over earnings.

The analysis in chapter 6 employs HMS household economy data in conjunction with demographic data from the MMP collected in 1994 and 1995. In the HMS, women are asked to identify all sources of income in the past month, and to provide the amount in dollars or pesos. Respondents are asked specifically whether they received income from children. This information can be linked to MMP data about the children who are in the United States to study the nature of the relationship between children's migration and cash transfers to parents. The HMS data do not identify comprehensively *which* children have provided income, so it is not possible to conclude that "Child X is in the United States and sent money to his parents in the month before interview." We are restricted to observing that some parents with adult children in the United States also receive cash transfers reported in dollars from children, and other do not.[21]

The HMS sample is less representative of Mexico than is the complete MMP sample, because data collection is restricted to a single state. To the extent that there are qualities unique to San Luis Potosí or to the process of migration between that state and the United States, the

---

[21] Household roster numbers are provided for up to two household/family members in the United States who sent money in the last month. Because some households have more than two members in the United States and because the value of the roster number is frequently coded to indicate "don't know," these data are not incorporated into the analysis.

results presented in chapter 6 will present a biased view of cash transfers from children to parents in Mexico.

Pros and Cons of Survey Data

The research questions posed in chapter 1 are analyzed over the next three chapters, using the survey data described above. The strength of social science survey data is the ability it gives researchers to identify patterns and distributions in large populations. In this research project, survey data enable an assessment of the relationship between migration and household change and a consideration of findings that are generalizable to comparable communities in central and western Mexico. However, survey data in general, and the MMP and HMS in particular, are lacking in several respects. As noted above, the data in the MMP are cross-sectional, with some retrospective data that permit discrete-time event history analysis. This design introduces at least two problems: first, there is no way to establish a direction of causality between two phenomena for which only cross-sectional data exist; and second, surveys requiring responses based on recollection are subject to respondent error. The HMS does allow a prospective study of the effects of remittance receipt on household well-being during a two-year time period, but the analysis is restricted to a single state. Another problem is that each survey relies on a single respondent to report on the behavior of all of the household members and children. This introduces a source of respondent error that potentially affects the current research, because much of the analysis pertains to household and family members other than the head or spouse. To address this potential source of error, I assume that respondent error on items pertaining to other household members is normally distributed, resulting in potentially inefficient but unbiased estimators.

Other problems occur more generally in survey data and quantitative analysis. A problem common to all analyses is unobserved heterogeneity, or the inability to control for everything that potentially influences the dependent variable. This introduces two concerns. First, observed effects might actually be the effects of other, unobserved variables. Second, conventional methods assume that the errors associated with the observed independent variables are independent and uncorrelated with the random error term in a statistical model. If the error terms are in fact correlated, the statistical model will produce biased results.

Another weakness of analyses that depend on survey data alone is that what they gain in generalizability, they lose in specificity and depth. The complexity of household structure and migration processes cannot easily be captured by quantitative measures, and resulting analyses can misread or overlook important data simply because it could not be incorporated into the framework of survey research. An array of qualitative and ethnographic research on migration and the family complements survey results and helps to guide and check quantitative research (Grasmuck and Pessar 1991; Hirsch 2003; Hondagneu-Sotelo 1994; Hondagneu-Sotelo 2001; Kanaiaupuni 1995).

These criticisms aside, the survey data used in this project are among the best sources available for studying migration processes on both sides of the Mexico-U.S. border. The MMP, in particular, has been used widely in the United States and Mexico by academics, policy researchers, and government agencies for its wealth of information on a process that is by its very nature difficult to track (Massey and Zenteno 2000). Many of the measures used in the quantitative analyses in this project have been published in peer-reviewed journals (Cerrutti and Massey 2001; Durand, Massey, and Zenteno 2001; Fussell and Massey 2004; Kanaiaupuni and Donato 1999; Massey and Espinosa 1997; Massey, Goldring, and Durand 1994; Stark and Taylor 1989), supporting the argument that these data are well-suited to a range of topics stemming from the study of U.S.-Mexico migration.

A DESCRIPTION OF PARENTAL HOUSEHOLDS IN MEXICO

For the current research, the MMP sample is limited to households in Mexico where the male head is currently in his first marriage or civil union and where he has at least one child. Data from households interviewed in the United States are excluded because the intent of the research is to consider the relationship between children's migration and the parental households that remain in Mexico. The restriction to male heads in marriages or civil unions permits the analysis of the effect of his spouse's education. Finally, focusing on heads in their first union permits the retrospective analysis of the effects of spouse's education and family size. (If the household head has been married or in a civil union previously, the education level for that spouse or

Table 3.2 Summary statistics for parental households in Mexico, MMP93

	Mean/ Proportion	Std. Dev.
Attributes of household head and spouse		
Household head's age	45.799	14.547
Household head's years of education	5.864	4.595
Household head's employment status		
Not in labor force	0.021	
Unemployed	0.062	
Employed	0.917	
Type of employment		
Agricultural work	0.306	
Unskilled non-agricultural work	0.542	
Skilled non-agricultural work	0.152	
Spouse's age	42.309	13.855
Spouse's years of education	5.541	4.083
Spouse's employment status		
Not in labor force	0.810	
Employed	0.190	
Attributes of parental household		
Household is in rural community	0.235	
Number of household residents	5.235	2.290
Number of workers in household	1.920	1.296
Number of non-workers in household	3.394	1.906
Household organization		
Nuclear	0.882	
Vertically extended	0.031	
Horizontally extended	0.056	
Other extended arrangement	0.073	
Number of sons in family	2.321	1.782
Number of adult sons in family	1.449	1.827
Number of daughters in family	2.291	1.798
Number of adult daughters in family	1.435	1.831
Adult children's average years of education	8.457	3.252
Number of minors in family	1.727	1.669

Table 3.2 Summary statistics for parental households in Mexico, continued

	Mean/ Proportion	Std. Dev.
Household assets		
Hectares owned by household	2.790	25.700
Hectares owned, given any ownership	14.869	57.811
Household head owns a business	0.235	
Household head owns home	0.715	
Migration experience in parental household		
Total number of U.S. trips taken	1.981	4.920
by current household members		
Number of adult sons in U.S.	0.251	0.773
Number of adult daughters in U.S.	0.119	0.502
Household head is in U.S.	0.039	
Household receives remittances	0.138	
Size of remittances, given any receipt*		
Small	0.478	
Medium	0.153	
Substantial	0.369	
Household receives remittances where	0.735	
head is in United States*		
Household receives remittances where any	0.504	
adult child is in United States*		

N=10,777 households

*N=2,594 households: Asked only of household heads interviewed since 1999.

partner is not recorded.) Restricting the analysis to household heads in their first union also prevents the need to model the effects of transitions in family structure. The exclusion of female-headed households and households where the head has had more than one spouse or partner potentially biases the analysis by ignoring variation in family structure, but over 80 percent of household heads who are parents are in their first union at the time of interview.

Table 3.2 summarizes descriptive statistics about the attributes of the parental household and the household head as well as migration experience in the household. On average, the household head is just under 46 years old, and has a little less than 6 years of school, equivalent to a primary school education. Over 90 percent of household heads are employed, and the majority of workers are engaged in unskilled, non-agricultural employment. Thirty percent of working heads are in agricultural work, and 15 percent are in skilled, non-agricultural employment. Six percent of heads are unemployed and actively seeking work. About two percent of men are out of the labor force, typically because they are retired or disabled.

The head's spouse is slightly younger than the head (42.3 years) and has about one-third of a year less of schooling. The majority of spouses, 81 percent, are out of the labor force. Further analysis not shown here indicates that women who are employed are slightly younger and more often reside in urban areas than women not in the labor force, but family size and the number of minors in the household are similar for working and non-working women.

On average, a household includes about five coresident members at the time of interview. Just under two household members are employed, and about 3.4 members are not working. About 88 percent of households are organized in a nuclear family structure with only parents and children coresiding. (This includes households with coresident adult children.) Three percent of households are vertically extended, meaning that members of a generation older than the household head reside in the home. These coresidents include the head's parents, parents-in-law, and aunts or uncles. In 5.6 percent of cases, the household is horizontally extended, meaning that members of the head's generation or his children's generation reside in the household, including cousins, brothers- and sisters-in-law, and sons- and daughters-in-law. About 7 percent of households are otherwise extended, including nieces or nephews, grandchildren, and other relatives or non-relatives. (The categories do not sum to 100 because households may be in more than one category.)

Household heads have 2.3 sons and 2.3 daughters, on average. This represents childbearing patterns from an earlier fertility regime in Mexico. (Currently, the total fertility rate is about 3 births per woman.) Just over half of the sons and daughters are adults at the time of interview, and households include about 1.7 minors. Adult children have an average of almost 8.5 years of education, nearly three years more than their parents had, reflecting a secular trend over time toward more years of schooling.

The household assets that are measured over time include home ownership, business ownership, and land ownership, so those are the assets considered in the analysis in subsequent chapters that rely on time-varying retrospective information. Over 70 percent of household heads own the home they reside in at the time of interview, and about a quarter of heads report owning a business. On average, households own 2.79 hectares of land, but among those who own any land, the average landholding is 14.9 hectares. Land ownership is more common in rural areas than in urban areas: Almost 43 percent of rural households own some land, compared to 11 percent of urban households (not shown in table).

Households have extensive migration experience. On average, almost two trips to the United States have been made by people living in the household at the time of interview, and .25 sons and .11 daughters are in the United States. Given that households include about 2.3 adult sons and a similar number of adult daughters, these figures suggest that about one in ten sons and one in twenty daughters is a current migrant. Furthermore, although the household remains based in Mexico, 3.9 percent of household heads are in the United States at the time of interview, meaning that his spouse or child is serving as a proxy respondent.

Almost 14 percent of households are connected to the migration experience through the receipt of remittances from the United States. (Note that these data are representative only for households interviewed since 1999.) Nearly half of remittance recipients report that they receive "small" amounts of money, but over one-third report receiving "substantial" amounts. The data do not indicate from whom the remittances were received, but in 73.5 percent of cases where the household head is in the United States, the proxy respondent reports receiving remittances. Where at least one adult child is in the United States, 50.4 percent of households report receiving remittances. (There is some overlap where household heads and children are in the United States at the same time, and it is not possible to infer who sent remittances, but restricting the analysis to cases where only the head or only adult children are abroad produces similar results to those shown here.)

This descriptive summary portrays a sample of households that is diverse in terms of composition, employment, urbanicity, and socioeconomic status. Adult children have relatively high education compared to their parents and a high prevalence of migration. The subsequent chapters evaluate how these parental households and the adult children raised there interact to incorporate international migration into family dynamics and processes.

CHAPTER 4

The Influence of Households of Origin on Mexico-U.S. Migration

Many Mexico-U.S. migrants begin their transnational careers as adult children in their parents' households. Yet the role of migrants in their households of origin, and the household's effect on an individual's likelihood of migration, have received relatively little attention. The propensity for children from the same household to migrate may vary as much as their roles and position in the family do. Why do some children migrate, while their siblings do not? In the context of the parental household, is children's migration behavior a consequence of demand and supply, of varying access to migration networks, or something else?

Households from the Mexican Migration Project (MMP) described in the previous chapter are analyzed in this chapter to determine who becomes a migrant among the adult children from a common parental household, and whether children from the same household are influenced in different ways to migrate. For example, gender and birth order may be associated with different migration chances for children from the same households, if these individual characteristics interact differently with household attributes.

A statistical model that includes attributes of individuals, households, and communities is developed to estimate the probability that an adult child initiates migration from Mexico to the United States and works in the United States. Models are computed separately for sons and daughters in urban and rural communities. The individual-level attributes taken into account include age, education, birth order, and migration experience within Mexico. Household-level factors include socioeconomic status, family size, the sex composition of the pool of adult children, and migration history among immediate family members. Community-level factors include the local male employment rate and the prevalence of migration experience.

Distinct processes within the household are expected to drive the migration of daughters who work in the United States compared to migrant daughters who do not join the U.S. labor force. For example, economic need may not play a strong role in predicting non-labor migration, compared to the importance of that factor in predicting labor migration. The statistical analysis provides a test of this hypothesis with a multinomial logistic regression that estimates the log-odds of a daughter migrating as a non-worker or migrating and working, compared to remaining in Mexico. For sons, a logistic regression provides estimates of the log-odds of any migration to the United States compared to remaining in Mexico. (The vast majority of male migrants work in the United States.) The analysis is based on retrospective person-year data from the first 10 years of the adult lives of children from the households included in the MMP.

The current analysis represents an empirical comparison of various migration theories within the context of the parental household. The analysis builds on previous comparisons of theories by testing interactions between children's standing in the household and other characteristics of the household, including socioeconomic status, life cycle stage, and migration history in order to assess whether different factors operate at various times to explain migration decisions.

PREDICTORS OF MIGRATION IN A HOUSEHOLD CONTEXT

The migration theories described in chapter 2 point to several predictors of migration that operate in sending households. First, neoclassical models predict that migrants travel in order to satisfy economic need. The new economics of migration adds to this perspective by considering relative economic need as well as absolute need. Second, migration studies conducted in the framework of the household recognize that potential migrants frequently rely on others to take up their household responsibilities in order to make a trip possible. Satisfying this need requires the availability of kin to carry out such roles. Third, social capital theory in the context of Mexico-U.S. migration predicts that people who have a network of friends and family with migration experience are more likely to migrate themselves. Each set of predictors is discussed in order below.

Economic need within the household is a powerful predictor of international labor migration. Even in contexts where social structure and social capital add explanatory power to empirical tests of migration theories, economic need continues to play a significant explanatory role (Massey et al. 1994). But neither absolute nor relative economic need remains the same in a household over time (Stark and Taylor 1989). The household dependency ratio is one example of changing absolute need. As households and families age, the dependency ratio follows a curvilinear pattern, with most of the dependency accounted for by minors early in the household life cycle, and by aging parents later. Household heads and older children will respond to economic need created by family size and dependency. As parents become dependents, the responsibility for their care may fall to younger children, whose independent life course trajectories may not be as well-established as those of their older siblings.

The data used in the current analysis permit a test of the concept of economic need several ways, using time-varying data. First, the number of consumers in the household who do not also contribute resources as producers represent dependency in the household. As the number of dependents increases (or as their numbers increase relative to the number of producers), economic need in the household also increases, causing greater pressure for at least one household member to migrate for work.

Second, the employment status and years of education of the household head and his spouse represent the extent to which they provide for the household through earnings. Women's education is also associated with the division of labor in the household and with the allocation of resources to children and other family members.

Third, socioeconomic status (SES) in the household indicates the wealth and resources potentially available to all household members, although not all members necessarily have access. Because of the volatility of the Mexican economy historically, SES is measured here by an index of assets, rather than by income or savings. The analysis also includes indicators of the years of education completed by the household head and the head's spouse.

Fourth, employment levels in the local labor force indicates the constraints and opportunities to which all working-age household members are exposed. Neoclassical theory would predict that where employment rates are high, children are less likely to migrate because they can take advantage of local opportunities.[22]

Availability of kin is another factor related to migration that varies *within* and *between* households. This availability includes other kin who can potentially migrate, as well as kin who can take over a migrant's role in the household or local labor force, as the household strategies model would predict. But not all kin are treated equally in the domains of the household, the labor force, and migration flows. In particular, gender and age are important attributes that affect how well one sibling, parent, or other relative can take the place of an absent household member. For example, a son who has only sisters will consider that if he migrates, his parents' household will be supported by siblings who will typically find work in the informal sector or in poorly paid positions in manufacturing. Those earnings may be less than what the son would earn in the formal labor market if he remained in Mexico. In contrast, the oldest daughter in the same household may feel that she can migrate and expect her younger sisters to take her place, providing comparable labor and income to what she would have produced in Mexico.

The availability of siblings may be measured by summing up separately the number of adult sons and adult daughters reported by the household head. Ideally, such a measure would also include time-varying information on whether these children resided in the head's household, as coresidence is strongly correlated with participation in

---

[22] Relative economic status compared to other households in the community is another indicator of economic need. The current analysis uses a person-year data file that requires time-varying information from each year that an adult child was between the ages of 15 and 25, a period that might fall any time between 1965 and the year of interview. Because we do not know how long each household in the sample has resided in the community where the interview takes place, it is not possible to develop a time-varying measure of relative economic status, so that indicator is excluded.

the household economy and activities but such information is not available in the data used here.

Migrants incur costs and risks when they initiate migration. These factors may be thought of as the *transaction costs* (Williamson 1979; Williamson 1981) associated with migrating. Potentially, these transaction costs can be reduced when migrants tap the **social capital** existing in their relationships with kin who have already begun migrating (see Massey et al. 1994; Massey and Espinosa 1997). Before elaborating how social capital operates to make migration easier, a review of transaction costs follows, with an explanation of why this approach is a suitable way to measure the benefits of social capital within households.

The notion of transaction costs was developed by economic theorists in order to identify the non-market reasons that explain when and why organizations make contracts with each other. The critical components of transaction costs that Williamson (Piore 1979) identified can be categorized as uncertainty, the frequency and complexity of transactions, and asset specificity, or the need for highly specific resources that are particular to a single type of investment. Proximity, a shared business history, or other conveniences shared between firms make the contract easier to implement, although there may be no difference in the financial costs proposed by two firms bidding with a third for a contract. When transaction costs are reduced, the exchange is more efficient, and therefore more desirable.

This approach has been extended to the sociology of the family to consider the economic organization of marriage (Treas 1993), where the actors are individuals, rather than institutions. In that case, "efficiency" is represented by an effort to minimize the frequency and hassle of negotiating exchanges like bill-paying. If bill-paying were a one-time event in which no one felt indebted to the bill payer and the bill payer could point to and quantify the benefits he received from paying the bills, that transaction might have no emotional or social cost, and responsibility for household finances could be delegated easily. But because bill-paying happens in the context of complex relationships, and because the benefits of maintaining a solvent household are neither discrete nor always quantifiable, the potential for conflict exists. To avoid that conflict, couples develop different strategies to make bill-paying more efficient. Those strategies depend not only on characteristics of economic exchange like earnings contributions, but on qualities particular to the familial relationship like trust and commitments to the family, as well as an authority structure and normative guidelines about relationships between kin (Treas 1993).

The concepts of transaction costs and efficiency emphasize the value of the social capital derived from within the family for migration. Like the transactions described, international migration is characterized by uncertainty and complexity, as well as by the need for a specific set of skills and resources. Potential migrants benefit from the information and support kin can provide to increase the chances of successful migration. Although a potential migrant may have many other resources within the sending community or in the receiving area, kin have a particular interest in ensuring the quality of the migration process for one another. This interest results from a shared membership in a family or household where relationships involve trust, love, and commitment, as well as from a sense of responsibility not only to the potential migrant, but to the remaining family members as well.

This sense of responsibility inheres within the household in part because of the concrete nature of the relationships there (Treas 1993). The tie between siblings or between parents and children will persist even if one party fails to hold up his end of a commitment, although that relationship may become more strained. Ties between community members or between extended kin, while potentially very strong, are more malleable because they lack the normative structure of familial relationships. As a result, the consequences of failing to satisfy the terms of an agreement may be less than they would within a family-based household, because both parties can redefine the nature of their relationship.

The quality of the social capital associated with siblings' migration potentially varies by the migrant's sex. Men and women will have different experiences as migrants in terms of their own access to social capital, their experience crossing the border and becoming established in the receiving country, their likelihood of working, and among those who find jobs, in the kind of work they do. These differences will result in distinct fields of knowledge and social networks. This analysis considers whether adult sons' and daughters' migration has different effects, if any, on their siblings' likelihood of migrating and working.

Demand and supply factors are expected to interact with social capital to give each child a different probability of migrating, based on the social and economic characteristics of the household at different points in time. Consider birth order as a possible source of variation within households. In a family with many children where economic factors determine the demand for labor, the oldest child will be expected to begin working relatively early, but the costs and risks associated with migration might be too high to sacrifice that source of immediate labor and income, so initial migration will be delayed. When younger children become adults, there are fewer dependents, and other siblings who have already begun migration will lower the associated risks and costs. Consequently, these adult children might initiate migration earlier if social capital prevails as the motivating force, or they might delay or reject migration if lower economic need in the household makes migration less critical as a diversified source of income.

Social capital also exists outside the parental household. At the community level, the cumulative experience of men and women who have migrated to the United States represents a store of specific knowledge about the migration experience and a wealth of connections to current migrants. However, access to that capital varies by the context of the community. A "culture of migration" (Kandel and Massey 2002) is more firmly established in rural areas, which have a long history of international migration compared to urban areas. The tradition of migration from rural areas and the proximity and intensity of social ties there compared to urban areas are reflected in a stronger influence of community-level migration rates on an individual's probability of becoming a migrant (Fussell and Massey 2004).

Quantitative analysis permits empirical tests of six hypotheses emerging from the preceding discussion:

- Households with greater economic need will be more likely to send sons and daughters to the United States to work.
- The availability of kin in households with more adult members will enable children to migrate.
- Households where more children have been to the United States already will be more likely to send other adult children as migrants.
- Children will be more influenced by the migration behavior of their same-sex siblings than by that of their opposite-sex siblings.
- Children in urban areas will be more influenced by their siblings' migration experience and less influenced by the

community-level   migration   experience,   vis-à-vis   adult
children in rural areas.

- If economic need prevails as the motivator of children's
  migration, younger children in the parental household will be
  less likely to migrate if siblings precede them as migrants. But
  if social capital is the driving force behind children's
  migration, younger siblings will be more likely to go when
  other siblings have already migrated.

DATA

The analysis draws on data from 88 of the 93 communities in the
Mexican Migration Project (MMP) that include spouses' occupational
histories to construct a person-year file for all of the children of the
household head who are at least age 18 by the age of interview.[23]
Because adulthood is often considered to begin at age 15 in research on
Mexico, the first record for each individual in the person-year file
begins at that age. The restriction to individuals who are at least 18 at
the time of interview allows us to observe their migration and work
behavior in the first three years of adulthood. Person-year data are
merged to a set of time-varying community-level demographic and
economic characteristics in order to obtain contextual data about
employment rates and the prevalence of migration in the sending
community. Observations are censored at the year of first migration,
the year in which the migrant is 25 years old, or the year of interview,
whichever comes first. Age 25 is used as a cutoff in order to focus on
the effects of households of origin on early adulthood only. The final
sample includes 214,432 person-years, representing the lives of 28,877
individuals.

Dependent Variables

For sons, the dependent variable includes only two categories: whether
the son took his first trip to the United States (coded 1) or remained in
Mexico (coded 0) in year *t*. For daughters, the dependent variable

---

[23] The remaining five communities are excluded because of concerns about
data quality.

includes three categories: whether she remained in Mexico (coded 0) in year *t;* whether she took her first trip to the United States but did not work there (coded 1) in year *t;* and whether she migrated to the United States and was employed there (coded 2) in year *t.*[24]

Independent Variables

All time-varying variables are lagged one year. That is, for all attributes that change over time, like the household head's employment status, the analysis uses information from year *t-1* to predict whether a child migrated in year *t.*

Age in years: Based on earlier research, the probability of migration is expected to peak in early adulthood and decline steadily after the early 20's. An age-squared term is included to capture this non-linear effect.[25]

---

[24] Work is defined as any reported activity carried out by a migrant in the labor force, i.e., not unemployed, a homemaker, a student, or a tourist. A more precise dependent variable would put children who remained in Mexico and worked there in a separate category from children who remained and were not employed. However, the available data lack complete time-varying information on children's employment. The interviewer collects information only on whether a child is working at the time of the interview, and if a child migrated (either internationally or within Mexico), in what year the child migrated and whether he or she worked during that trip. As a result, it is impossible to determine whether a nonmigrant child was employed in any year before the interview.

[25] Age is computed as the difference between the survey year and the adult child's year of birth. Because of multiple sources of error, including respondent error, interviewer error, and data entry error, there are about 100 cases where the child of the household head is fewer than 12 years younger than his parent. (In fact, in some cases, the adult child is *older* than his parent.) This seemingly implausible outcome may be the result of errors pertaining to the reported year of birth or the reported relationship between the head and household member. In the absence of other information, I made the decision to remove those adult children from the data set who were reportedly fewer than 12 years younger than their parent.

Years of education: An increase in education is expected to be associated with a declining risk of labor migration for men, but an increasing risk for women. This expectation is based on prior research that indicates Mexican women see greater returns to education in the United States because of a strongly sex-segregated occupational distribution in Mexico (Kanaiaupuni and Fomby 2000).

Whether child has ever migrated within Mexico: Children's internal migration experience may be positively related with U.S. migration and work, if children are moving north in stages (White 1994); or internal migration experience may divert children away from U.S. migration streams if they have found work elsewhere in Mexico.

Birth order: Birth order is expected to affect how adult children stand in relation to other household characteristics. Of particular interest is how birth order interacts with the prevalence of migration experience in the household. This effect is captured through an interaction term.

Employment status of household head: Children are expected to be more likely to migrate where the household head is unemployed or out of the labor force.

Household head's years of completed education: Apart from the head's current employment status, his education level is indicative of his potential earning capacity. To the extent that children's migration is motivated by economic need, more years of education achieved by the household head is expected to reduce the likelihood of children's migration. The analysis uses a continuous measure of years of education, with a range from 0 to 23 years.

Spouse's years of completed education: The spouse's years of education may operate as an indicator of human capital in the same way as the head's years of education. Alternatively, her years of education may be associated with a higher likelihood of daughters' migration if women's higher education is associated with a more equitable distribution of resources to children. The continuous measure of spouse's years of education ranges from 0 to 22.

Spouse's cumulative months of work experience: The spouse's labor force experience is another indicator of human capital. Women's prior work experience is also associated with greater power and autonomy in the household. In turn, the likelihood of migration is expected to be more equal for sons and daughters if women's employment is associated with a more equal distribution of investments in children's migration. Work experience is measured in months and then logged to produce a less skewed distribution.[26]

Number of adult children in the family: The number of children age 15 or over represents the kin available to the household for labor and income. Adult brothers and adult sisters are counted in separate measures.

Number of minors in the family: The number of children under age 15 represents the minimum number of dependents in the household.

Parental household wealth: A socioeconomic status (SES) index scored 0 to 3 measures whether the household head owns the household's residence (coded 1, 0 otherwise); whether the household head owns a business (coded 1, 0 otherwise); and whether the household owns at least 5 hectares of land (coded 1, 0 otherwise) (Donato and Kanaiaupuni 2000).[27] A higher SES index is expected to positively predict migration, because families with more resources can better afford the absence of one child.

Number of siblings ever in the United States: The number of an adult child's brothers or sisters who have ever migrated to the United States is expected to be positively associated with a child's likelihood of migration. Brothers and sisters are counted separately.

Community-level male migration prevalence: Adult children from communities in which migration has become "institutionalized" are expected to have a greater likelihood of migrating, both because of available instrumental support and because of relevant social norms, particularly in rural areas. In urban areas, migration experience has not

---

[26] Cumulative experience, rather than current employment status, is used. A positive association between current employment status and children's migration would be difficult to interpret because women's employment might represent greater economic need or it might represent a looser division of labor need in the household. Women's employment history may be indicative of household organization without introducing the alternative interpretation of current economic need.

[27] Donato and Kanaiaupuni's (2000) measure of SES included several measures of housing quality, but that information is not available for homes occupied prior to the date of interview. They also counted landholdings separately outside of the index.

saturated the local culture to the same extent, and migration prevalence is less predictive of migration (Fussell and Massey 2004). The influence of the community-level migration prevalence gives us a benchmark against which to assess the relative importance of siblings' migration, which may be greater in urban areas.

Community-level male employment rate: Neoclassical economic theories predict that higher employment rates locally deter an adult child's migration.

Historical time: The analysis considers the likelihood of migration between 1965 and 2002. The years are grouped into four periods. The first, from 1965 to 1979, covers the post-Bracero era, when undocumented migration to the United States first began to increase. The second, from 1980 to 1987, represents a period of economic instability in Mexico and captures the implementation of the 1986 Immigration Reform and Control Act (IRCA). The third period, from 1988 to 1995, represents the post-IRCA era and the first few years after which immigrants legalized by IRCA would have become eligible for citizenship. During the last period, 1996 to 2002, migration had become institutionalized in some sending communities. At the same time, state and federal policies in the United States evolved to discourage migration by denying services to both undocumented and documented migrants. The probability of migration is expected to increase over historical time, particularly after the passage of the 1986 Immigration Reform and Control Act (IRCA).

DESCRIPTIVE ANALYSIS

Table 4.1 presents sample means and frequencies for the characteristics described above. The figures in the table are presented in person-years. In a person-year data file, each observation represents one year lived by a person in the sample. For example, if 10 people were observed for 10 years, there would be 100 person-year records in the analysis file. In table 4.1, information is presented separately for nonmigrant and migrant person-years. There are many more nonmigrant person-years than migrant person-years for two reasons. First, most people never migrated between the time they were 15 and 25 years old. Second, among those who did eventually migrate, in most years they were still nonmigrants. For example, a son who migrated for the first time at age

Table 4.1 Unweighted means and frequencies, independent variables, MMP93

	Non-migrant person-years		Migrant person-years		
	Mean	SD	Mean		SD
Child's characteristics					
Male	0.477		0.733	*	
Age	19.180	3.088	19.426	*	2.735
Years of education	7.298	3.541	7.216	*	2.979
Birth order	3.720	2.504	3.995	*	2.552
Ever migrated within Mexico	0.041		0.037		
Number of brothers ever in the U.S.	0.307	0.770	0.855	*	1.177
Number of sisters ever in the U.S.	0.100	0.415	0.330	*	0.772
Household characteristics					
Rural residence (<2500 people)	0.255		0.423	*	
Head's years of education	3.669	3.696	2.847	*	2.888
Spouse's years of education	3.733	3.241	3.280	*	2.697
Head is employed	0.958		0.965	*	
Socioeconomic status index (0-3)	1.064	0.710	1.133	*	0.727
Number of minors	2.619	2.260	2.714	*	2.268

Table 4.1 Unweighted means and frequencies, independent variables, MMP93, continued

	Non-migrant person-years		Migrant person-years	
	Mean	SD	Mean	SD
Number of adult sons	2.311	1.749	2.768 *	1.723
Number of adult daughters	2.323	1.745	2.322	1.772
Household head in United States	0.058		0.159 *	
Community characteristics				
Male employment rate	0.658	0.155	0.642 *	0.176
Proportion of men with U.S. migration	0.284	0.192	0.448 *	0.204
experience				
Period				
1965-1979	0.242		0.215 *	
1980-1987	0.325		0.315	
1988-1995	0.328		0.379 *	
1996-2002	0.028		0.027	
N (person-years)	210,277		4,155	

*Group differences are statistically significant at p<.05

22 is counted in the sample for eight years – the seven years between age 15 and age 21 when he was a nonmigrant, and the one year when he went to the United States. After that, he is removed from the analysis file, because he is no longer at risk for becoming a first-time migrant.

Adult migrant children and their households are different from children who remain in Mexico in ways that are relevant to the theories that have been elaborated. The availability of more adult children in migrant-sending parental households indicates that kin may assume the local workload that a migrant child leaves behind. The much higher prevalence of recent migration by siblings and by the household head, the higher proportion of men in the community with U.S. migration experience, and the relative concentration of migrants in later periods compared to nonmigrants suggest the importance of social capital and cumulative causation. The picture is less clear for how economic need influences children's migration. Lower parental education, the slightly higher number of minors in the household, and lower male employment rates in the community in migrant person-years point to a demand for diverse sources of income support from adult children. But the employment status of the household head is similar for migrant and nonmigrant children. Migrant-sending parental households have a slightly higher socioeconomic status index, suggesting that those households either are better equipped to pay the costs of migration (both material costs and opportunity costs) relative to those who do not migrate, or household members realize greater demand to raise the absolute standard of living.

Other distinctions also merit attention. As expected, most migrants are male and migrants have slightly less education than nonmigrants. About 4.1 percent of international migrants have internal migration experience, compared to 3.7 percent for nonmigrants. This difference suggests that in the population considered, children's U.S.-bound migration is an alternative to migration within Mexico, rather than the end result of a stage migration process, which would be characterized by a series of sequential moves beginning within Mexico.

Theories regarding the distribution of resources in parental households have generated hypotheses about a causal relationship between a mother's education and her children's more equitable access to resources by gender. In this subsample of the MMP, the mothers of children who migrate have slightly more education than their husbands, while the mothers of nonmigrant children have less. Mothers of migrant children may have been able to leverage the greater human capital associated with higher education to enable their children's migration. Additional analysis (not shown here) indicates that migrant daughters are no more likely than migrant sons to have mothers with more education than fathers.

Figure 4.1 compares the proportion of adult children in the sample migrating in any year by their family size and by family migration history.[28] The lower two lines show the differences in the number of migrants by family size and by birth order rank. The line marked by squares shows that there is a monotonic increase in migration frequencies associated with family size. Almost 20 percent of children from families with 10 children migrate by age 25, compared to only 3 percent of children in families with only one or two children. The comparison by birth order is less striking, but still significant. The line marked by diamonds indicates that about 10 percent of first-born adult children become migrants, compared to 14 percent of children between parity 6 and parity 9. The higher proportion of migrants among higher birth order children suggests that migration is not merely a response to pressure resulting from family size, because by the time higher birth order children become adults, many siblings have preceded them in labor force entry, marriage, and homeleaving. One interpretation that arises when these patterns are considered jointly is that adult children's migration is a strategy undertaken by younger children in large households in order to diversify income sources after older children have begun earning income in Mexico. This interpretation supports two explanations of children's migration, the availability of kin and economic need.

The top two lines in figure 4.1 indicate the differences in the proportion of children migrating by the migration experiences of their siblings. The difference between having no migrant siblings and having even one is stark. Only 4 percent of adult children migrate by age 25

---

[28] The data for figure 4.1 are drawn from the households used in the multivariate analysis that follows. A migrant is defined as an adult child from the household who migrated for the first time any time between age 15 and age 25.

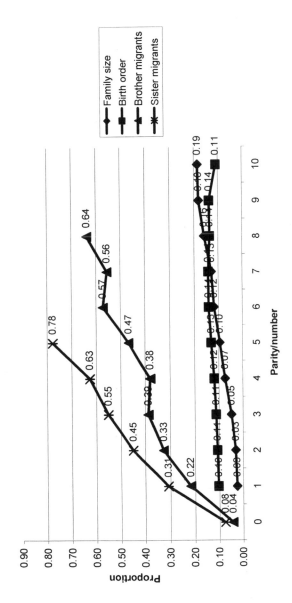

Figure 4.1
Proportion of adult children who migrated in any year by family size and family migration history

Source: MMP93

73

when they have no brothers with migration experience, but when one brother has already initiated migration, 22 percent of adult children also migrate. The frequency of migration continues to rise almost monotonically as the number of migrant siblings rises. The relationship between migration frequency and sisters' migration appears even stronger than the relationship with brothers' migration, suggesting that sisters' migration occurs in households where migration is institutionalized. The observed patterns suggest that the availability of social capital within the household and the process of cumulative causation make migration easier and more common among siblings once at least one child has begun to migrate.

Table 4.2 shows the frequency of migration for sons and daughters in rural and urban areas. The figures represent the incidence of first migration over the 11-year period when a child is between the ages of 15 and 25. To interpret the figures, consider the example provided earlier, with a person-year file with 100 observations representing 10 years lived by 10 people. If 5 of the people migrate in the tenth year they are observed, the incidence of migration will be 5 events/(10 people x 10 years)=5/100, or 5 percent.

Rural sons were the most frequent migrants, with a first migration event occurring in 4.8 percent of the person-years under observation. Urban sons migrated in 2.3 percent of person-years, or less than half as often. Rural daughters migrated in 1.6 percent of person-years, and urban daughters about half as often. Among migrants sons, employment in the United States was nearly universal. More than 98 percent of rural sons and more than 96 percent of urban sons worked. Migrants daughters were about equally likely to work or to not work, although rural daughters worked slightly more often than urban daughters. The proportions working in the United States were 59.8 percent and 50.6 percent, respectively.

MULTIVARIATE ANALYSIS

Discrete-time regression models based on the person-year data file described in table 4.1 estimate the probability that a child becomes a migrant. The sample is divided into four groups: sons in rural communities (<2500 residents), rural daughters, sons in urban areas, and urban daughters. The division by gender and urbanicity addresses

Table 4.2 Incidence of migration by gender and urbanicity, MMP93

	Rural Sons	Urban Sons	Rural Daughters	Rural Daughters
Not in the United States in year t	0.951	0.977	0.984	0.992
In the United States in year t	0.048	0.023	0.016	0.008
Of those in U.S., proportion not working	0.013	0.038	0.402	0.494
Of those in U.S., proportion working	0.987	0.962	0.598	0.506
N (person-years)	26,097	77,197	29,347	81,791
N (number of children)	3,939	10,548	3,856	10,544

75

the distinctive processes that drive migration in each context. The model uses robust standard errors to account for the fact that observations within households are not independent.

The models estimating sons' and daughters' migration probabilities have different dependent variables and use slightly different statistical methods as a result. As table 4.2 shows, very few sons migrated to the United States and did not work, but only about half of migrant daughters were employed in the United States. Therefore, the model predicting daughters' migration distinguishes between labor migration and other migration, while the model predicting sons' migration assumes all migrant sons were employed. For sons, the resulting model is a logistic regression that estimates the log-odds of a child's migration to the United States in a given year compared to remaining in Mexico, given that he has not migrated in any previous year. For daughters, a multinomial logistic regression estimates the log-odds of migrating and not working or migrating and working in a given year compared to remaining in Mexico, given that she has not migrated in any previous year.

The models are centered at parity three (the third-oldest child in the household) (Aiken and West 1991). In other words, these models estimate the effects of the predictors on the probability of migration where an observed person-year is lived by the third child born in the household. If the predictors were not centered on birth order, the other coefficients in the model would pertain to an individual with birth order 0. Obviously, it is impossible to be the 0th child born in a household, so that starting point is not meaningful. Parity 3 is the modal birth order ranking of adult children in the sample. To interpret statistical results, it is useful to consider the effects of departing from this average.

The statistical results are presented as odds ratios.[29] Odds are defined as the ratio between the probability of an event occurring (p) and the probability of the event not occurring (1-p). Odds are denoted below by the symbol Ω. The odds ratio is a ratio between the odds of an event occurring when all of the independent variables in an equation (collectively referred to as **x**) take on a certain value and the odds of

---

[29] Coefficients in the statistical model are computed as log-odds, or the logged value of the odds ratios. The coefficients have been converted to odds ratios for ease of interpretation.

that event occurring when the value of a single independent variable in the equation, variable x_k, changes by quantity δ. To compare the odds before and after adding δ to x_k, we take the odds ratio (Long 1997):

$$\text{Odds Ratio}= \frac{\Omega(\mathbf{x}, x_k + \delta)}{\Omega(\mathbf{x}, x_k)}$$

The odds ratio may be interpreted as the factor by which the odds of an event increase or decrease for a change of δ in x_k when the values of all other variables in the equation are unchanged.

For ease of interpretation, the odds ratio associated with a change of δ in x_k may be converted to a discrete change in the predicted probability of an event occurring. The probability may be expressed as (Long and Freese 2001):

$$\frac{\Delta \Pr(y = 1 \mid \mathbf{x})}{\Delta x_k} = \Pr(y = 1 \mid \mathbf{x}, x_k + \delta) - \Pr(y = 1 \mid \mathbf{x}, x_k)$$

A discrete change in the probability for a given change in the value of an independent variable assumes that the values of all other independent variables are held constant. In the results that follow, a discrete change in the probability is reported for a one-unit change in the value of each independent variable when all other variables are held at their means. For continuous variables, the one-unit change is treated as a change in the value from one-half of a point below the variable's mean to one-half of a point above the variable's mean. For dichotomous variables, the one-unit change is a change from a value of 0, indicating the absence of the characteristic, to a value of 1, indicating the presence of the characteristic.

Table 4.3 presents results from separate models for children from rural and urban communities to estimate the odds of sons' migration in any given year between age 15 and age 25. The first and third columns present odds ratios for rural sons and urban sons, respectively. The second and fourth columns present changes in the marginal probability of migration given a one-unit increase in the value of an individual independent variable over its mean for nonmigrants. The models include indicators of economic need, the availability of kin, and the

Table 4.3 Logistic regressions predicting whether an adult son ever migrated to United States, by urbanicity. MMP93

	Rural Men			Urban Men		
	OR	SE	change in p	OR	SE	change in p
Child's characteristics						
Age in years	5.982	1.065**	0.0597	4.920	0.644**	0.0244
Age squared	0.956	0.004**	-0.0014	0.961	0.003**	-0.0006
Years of education	1.003	0.011	0.0001	0.947	0.008**	-0.0006
Birth order (centered at 3)	0.923	0.041	-0.0025	0.898	0.029**	-0.0015
Ever migrated within Mexico	0.825	0.130	-0.0054	0.890	0.130	-0.0016
No. of brothers ever in U.S.	1.838	0.104**	0.0194	2.138	0.111**	0.0108
No. of sisters ever in U.S.	1.060	0.053	0.0018	1.237	0.083**	0.0030
Household characteristics						
No. of minors (<15) in household	1.044	0.020*	0.0013	1.075	0.016**	0.0010
Number of adult brothers in household	0.865	0.040	-0.0044	1.027	0.034	0.0004
Number of adults sisters in household	1.097	0.049*	0.0028	1.110	0.037**	0.0015
Household head is employed	0.894	0.215	-0.0035	1.081	0.153	0.0011
Household socioeconomic status	0.936	0.044	-0.0021	1.050	0.043	0.0007
Household head's years of education	1.018	0.017	0.0005	0.980	0.011	-0.0003
Spouse's years of education	1.019	0.019	0.0006	0.994	0.012	-0.0001
Household head ever in U.S.	1.458	0.137**	0.0114	1.604	0.169**	0.0066

Table 4.3 Logistic regressions predicting whether an adult son ever migrated to United States, by urbanicity, MMP93, continued

	Rural Men			Urban Men		
	OR	SE	change in p	OR	SE	change in p
Brother ever in U.S.*Birth order	0.969	0.009**	-0.0010	0.938	0.009**	-0.0009
Community characteristics						
Community-level male employment rate	0.957	0.194	-0.0013	0.628	0.124*	-0.0065
Male migration prevalence (vs. lowest quartile)						
2nd quartile	1.951	0.413**	0.0244	2.428	0.308**	0.0156
3rd quartile	4.136	0.777**	0.0639	3.845	0.474**	0.0274
4th quartile	7.178	1.371**	0.0882	6.277	0.793**	0.0497
Period (vs. 1980-1987)						
1965-1979	1.196	0.100	0.0031	0.810	0.060**	-0.0028
1988-1995	1.228	0.094**	0.0064	1.108	0.069	0.0015
1996-2002	1.056	0.204	0.0017	1.319	0.214	0.0044
Observations	26097			77197		

Robust standard errors are reported.

* significant at 5%; ** significant at 1%

79

availability of migration-related social capital in the household and in the community. Age, education, and birth order are included as sociodemographic controls. The results can be interpreted as the effect of a one-unit change in *x* on the odds (or the probability) that a child will migrate in a given year *t*.

Economic need. Among the household-level indicators of absolute need, coefficients are in the expected direction. The number of minor children in the parental household positively predicts sons' migration in both rural and urban parental households: the odds ratio is 1.044 for sons from rural areas and 1.075 for sons from urban areas. Put another way, each additional dependent child increases the odds of an adult.child's migration by 4.4 or 7.5 percent. The odds ratios translate to an increase in the probability of migration of .0013 for rural men and increase of .001 for urban men. For example, if the probability of migrating in a given year for rural sons is .029, the addition of a minor child in the household increases that probability by 4.4 percent, or .0013. Although this is a relatively small change in magnitude, the probability of migrating in any single year is low to begin with, and the annual probability of migrating cumulates over the 11-year period under observation. Over 11 years, the addition of one minor over the mean would represent a cumulative increase in the probability of migration of .0143.

The odds of migrating in a given year decrease as the community-level employment rate rises in urban areas only. In urban areas, an increase in the employment rate from .5 below the mean to .5 over the mean is associated with a change in the probability of sons' migration of -.0065. The rural/urban distinction may reflect the more advanced stage of cumulative causation in rural areas compared to urban areas, such that the process of migration has developed a logic and culture that operates independent of other conditions like economic need, which originally motivated the desire to migrate.

The other measures of economic need in the household are not significant. These include the household's socioeconomic status as measured by an index of assets, the employment status of the household head, and the education level of the head and his spouse. These many indicators were included to capture the multidimensional quality of economic need, including factors that may change quickly, like work status, and others that change more slowly, like asset accumulation. The results suggest that demand for resources, as represented by the number of minors in the household, is the most important indicator of economic need to influence children's migration probabilities.

It is noteworthy that the years of education of the household head's spouse does not have an independent effect on the odds of sons' migration when the education and employment status of the household head are controlled for. Beyond speaking to the household's socioeconomic status, this attribute was expected to represent the extent to which mothers translated their own human capital into power in the household in order to distribute migration-related material resources to their children. The statistical results indicate that sons from different families are equally likely to migrate whether their mothers are poorly or well educated.

Availability of kin. For both rural and urban sons, the number of adult sisters from the parental household positively predicts migration. For rural sons, the addition of an adult sister increases the probability of migration by .0028, and for urban sons by .0015. The number of adult brothers available has a negative and statistically weaker predictive effect on rural sons' migration only. This suggests that availability of kin contributes to sons' migration, but not because it represents the direct substitution of labor. That is, when one son migrates, the household may not draw directly on the immediate labor supply that another brother provides to replace him. Rather, the availability of daughters is more important. Daughters may provide a more flexible labor supply by entering the labor force or working more hours when sons migrate, while all sons are expected to work, regardless of whether their brothers migrate.

The interpretation is limited by an important caveat. The raw count of brothers and sisters is a rather crude measure of kin availability. It limits our ability to consider a more sophisticated relationship between kin, the division of household labor, and migration. As described in chapter 3, MMP data lack retrospective information on children's marriage and exits from the parental household. Therefore, it is not possible to obtain a measure of availability that distinguishes between those likely to provide assistance to the parental household and those who are not likely, like married children living in separate households.

Social capital. The availability of social capital within the household, as measured by siblings' migration prevalence, also positively predicts adult sons' migration. Brothers' prior U.S. migration has a strong positive influence on the log-likelihood of sons' migration. The odds of migration increase by 1.838 for sons in rural areas and by 2.138 for sons in rural areas when one brother has U.S. experience. These odds ratios represent marginal changes in the probability of migration of .0194 and .0108, respectively. The migration history of sisters also has a positive and significant effect on a son's odds of migrating in urban areas, but the magnitude of the effect is much smaller: the odds ratio is only about 60 percent of that for brothers' migration history. The magnitude and significance of these associations suggest the successful transmission of social capital within the parental household between siblings, but also indicate that the pathways for that transmission may be gender-specific, with men more strongly influenced by the behavior of their brothers than that of their sisters.

The main effects for brothers' migration history pertain to third-born children in a parental household. The model includes an interaction term that assesses the change in the effect of brothers' migration to the United States when a child's birth order rank increases or decreases. In both rural and urban areas, higher-birth order children with brothers who have migrated to the United States are *less likely* to become migrants than are lower birth order children or children with no migrant brothers. In rural areas, the odds of migration are reduced by about 3 percent for a son who is fourth-born when he has one brother who has been to the United States, and by 6 percent when two have been (OR=.964). In urban areas, the odds are further diminished, so that for the same son in an urban community, the odds of migration are reduced by 6 percent with one brother ever abroad and 12 percent with two brothers ever abroad.

The prevalence of migration experience in the community is measured in quartiles. The comparison group is children from households in communities in the lowest quartile. In each successive quartile, the odds of a son's migration is greater than in the last, so that for a child from a rural community in the top quartile, the odds of migrating are seven times higher than for a child from a community in the bottom quartile. For children from urban communities, the pattern is the same, but less dramatic. Still, a child from an urban community in the top quartile is six times as likely as a child from a community in the lowest quartile to become a migrant.

The direct comparison of children from rural and urban communities allows a comparison of the relative effects of migration by siblings and community members. Consistent with Fussell and Massey (2004), the current analysis shows that more migration experience in rural communities has a stronger influence on a son's odds of migrating than in urban areas. Conversely, migration by brothers and sisters in urban households has a stronger influence than in urban areas.

Table 4.4 shows the results of the model estimating daughters' migration. The analysis compares the odds of migrating to the United States without working (non-labor migration) or migrating and working (labor migration) to remaining in Mexico.[30] Overall, the pattern of results is distinctive from that for sons. Economic need does not appear to be as strong a motivator of daughter's migration. The number of minors in the parental household does not predict labor or non-labor migration, and higher SES is negatively associated with rural daughters' non-labor migration only. There are some differences among daughters by migration type. Where the household head is employed, daughters from rural communities are less likely to become non-labor migrants compared to households where the head is not employed. Among daughters from urban communities, father's years of education is negatively associated with labor migration. The community level male employment rate is not predictive of daughter's labor or non-labor migration.

The education of the spouse of the household head is not associated with daughters' migration chances. Research on the household power dynamics has hypothesized that the distribution of resources between sons and daughters is more equitable where mothers have greater-than-average human capital or contribute substantial earnings to the household economy, and empirical research in Mexico has found support for this hypothesis in regard to children's health and diet in middle-income households. However, the current analysis suggests that the hypothesis does not extend to the distribution of

---

[30] The logistic model predicting sons' migration produces odds ratios, but the multinomial logistic model of daughters' migration and work produces conditional odds ratios. The conditional odds ratio pertains to the situation where the dependent variable has more than two levels (Gould 2000). For the sake of simplicity, the results of the models of daughters' migration are described as odds ratios rather than as conditional odds ratios.

Table 4.4 Multinomial logistic regression predicting whether an adult daughter ever traveled to United States as non-labor or labor migrant, by urbanicity. MMP93

| | Rural Women | | | | | |
| | Non-labor Migration | | | Labor Migration | | |
	OR	SE	Change in p	OR	SE	Change in p
Child's characteristics						
Age in years	3.775	1.569**	0.0048	3.042	1.021**	0.0066
Age squared	0.969	0.010**	-0.0001	0.972	0.008**	-0.0001
Years of education	0.990	0.028	<.0001	1.031	0.022	0.0002
Birth order (centered at 3)	1.119	0.092	0.0004	0.918	0.076	-0.0005
Ever migrated within Mexico	0.114	0.115*	-0.0033	1.067	0.354	0.0004
No. of brothers ever in U.S.	1.258	0.102**	0.0008	1.283	0.098**	0.0014
No. of sisters ever in U.S.	2.188	0.274**	0.0027	2.420	0.230**	0.0052
Household characteristics						
No. of minors (<15) in household	0.931	0.042	-0.0002	1.047	0.034	0.0003
Number of adult brothers in household	0.798	0.069**	-0.0007	1.020	0.097	0.0001
Number of adults sisters in household	0.888	0.082	-0.0004	0.987	0.085	<.0001
Household head is employed	0.461	0.171*	-0.0039	0.820	0.342	-0.0012
Household socioeconomic status	0.764	0.087*	-0.0009	0.928	0.076	-0.0004
Household head's years of education	1.044	0.039	0.0001	1.050	0.036	0.0003
Spouse's years of education	1.043	0.047	0.0001	1.034	0.041	0.0003

Table 4.4 Multinomial logistic regression predicting whether an adult daughter ever traveled to United States as non-labor or labor migrant, by urbanicity, MMP93, continued

	Rural Women					
	Non-labor Migration			*Labor Migration*		
	OR	SE	Change in *p*	OR	SE	Change in *p*
Household head ever in U.S.	1.683	0.318**	0.0022	1.959	0.321**	0.0051
Sister ever in U.S.*Birth order	0.920	0.026**	-0.0003	0.951	0.016**	-0.0003
Community characteristics						
Community-level male employment rate	1.157	0.522	0.0005	0.762	0.313	-0.0016
Male migration prevalence (vs. lowest quartile)						
2nd quartile	3.611	2.186*	0.0069	1.846	0.865	0.0042
3rd quartile	9.170	4.886**	0.0164	4.964	2.068**	0.0153
4th quartile	10.170	5.332**	0.0117	6.095	2.464**	0.0135
Period (vs. 1980-1987)						
1965-1979	1.054	0.246	0.0002	1.413	0.276	0.0022
1988-1995	1.669	0.302**	0.0019	1.247	0.202	0.0013
1996-2002	1.408	0.669	0.0014	0.766	0.335	-0.0014
Observations	29347					

Table 4.4 Multinomial logistic regression predicting whether an adult daughter ever traveled to United States as non-labor or labor migrant, by urbanicity. MMP93, continued

	Urban Women					
	Non-labor Migration			Labor Migration		
	OR	SE	Change in p	OR	SE	Change in p
Child's characteristics						
Age in years	2.832	0.874**	0.0024	0.452	1.299**	0.0039
Age squared	0.969	0.010**	<.0001	0.972	0.008**	<.0001
Years of education	0.977	0.019	<.0001	1.022	0.019	<.0001
Birth order (centered at 3)	0.894	0.064	-0.0003	0.945	0.062	-0.0001
Ever migrated within Mexico	0.795	0.290	-0.0005	0.575	0.200	-0.0010
No. of brothers ever in U.S.	1.388	0.099**	0.0008	1.588	0.120**	0.0011
No. of sisters ever in U.S.	2.496	0.292**	0.0022	2.537	0.325**	0.0023
Household characteristics						
No. of minors (<15) in household	0.955	0.035	-0.0013	1.050	0.034	0.0023
Number of adult brothers in household	1.037	0.077	<.0001	0.870	0.071	-0.0003
Number of adults sisters in household	1.028	0.077	<.0001	1.003	0.070	<.0001
Household head is employed	0.901	0.224	-0.0003	0.983	0.273	<.0001
Household socioeconomic status	1.081	0.103	0.0002	1.267	0.120	0.0006
Household head's years of education	1.039	0.023	<.0001	0.952	0.023*	-0.0001
Spouse's years of education	1.028	0.029	0.0001	1.009	0.027	<.0001

Table 4.4 Multinomial logistic regression predicting whether an adult daughter ever traveled to United States as non-labor or labor migrant, by urbanicity, MMP93, continued

	Urban Women					
	Non-labor Migration			Labor Migration		
	OR	SE	Change in p	OR	SE	Change in p
Household head ever in U.S.	1.585	0.328*	0.0013	1.911	0.380**	0.0021
Sister ever in U.S.*Birth order	0.936	0.023**	-0.0002	0.892	0.023**	-0.0003
Community characteristics						
Community-level male employment rate	1.677	0.961	0.0012	0.893	0.349	-0.0003
Male migration prevalence (vs. 1st quartile)						
2nd quartile	1.598	0.405	0.0012	2.293	0.598**	0.0025
3rd quartile	2.700	0.657**	0.0030	2.780	0.713**	0.0032
4th quartile	6.055	1.421**	0.0079	4.289	1.097**	0.0057
Period (vs. 1980-1987)						
1965-1979	1.330	0.239	0.0007	1.032	0.188	<.0001
1988-1995	1.488	0.204**	0.0010	1.243	0.181	0.0005
1996-2002	1.218	0.518	0.0005	0.956	0.385	-0.0001
Observations	81791					

Robust standard errors are reported.

* significant at 5%; ** significant at 1%

migration-related resources among adult children in Mexican households.

The availability of kin as measured by the number of adult brothers or sisters from the parental household does not influence daughters' labor or non-labor migration, with the exception of the positive effect of number of brothers on rural daughters' non-labor migration. This is distinct from sons' migration, where the availability of daughters from the household positively predicts migration.

Consistent with sons' migration, the likelihood of daughters' migration is increased by the earlier migration of brothers and sisters to the United States. In contrast to sons' migration, daughters are much more influenced by their sisters' migration than by their brothers'. The earlier migration of one sister increases the odds of a daughter's labor or non-labor migration by more than two times compared to having no sisters with migration experience.

Parallel to the model of sons' migration, the direct effect for sisters' migration experience pertains to a third-born child. The interaction term between birth order and sisters' migration experience indicates that younger daughters are less likely to become migrants when at least one sister has been a migrant in the past. The consistency in the direction and magnitude of the interaction coefficient across types of migration suggest that lower migration probabilities among younger children emerge from a cultural expectation that younger adult children will remain in the parental household. We might conclude that between higher birth order and sisters' migration experience derived from economic need if the coefficient were negative and significant only in predicting labor migration,.

The influence of the community-level prevalence of male migration experience follows a similar pattern for daughters and sons. The positive influence on daughters' migration is stronger in rural areas than in urban areas, and is stronger in predicting labor migration than non-labor migration, except at the highest quartile for urban women. The effect of male migration experience on the odds of migration is lower for daughters from urban areas than for sons, but for daughters and sons from rural areas, the size of the effect is comparable in predicting labor migration.

DISCUSSION

This research was guided by questions about how households of origin influence adult children's initial migration to the United States. Six hypotheses were presented and evaluated through descriptive and multivariate analysis. The hypotheses are reviewed and discussed below.

Hypothesis 1. Households with greater economic need will be more likely to send sons and daughters to the United States to work. A variety of indicators of economic need were considered together. The number of minor children in the parental household was strongly associated with sons' labor migration. Other indicators included parental education and employment and the household's socioeconomic status as measured by an index of assets. This comparison of the influence of the various dimensions of economic need supports the argument that at least for sons, children's migration is tied to the life course of the parental household such that the probability of migration drops when there are fewer dependents demanding financial resources.

Hypothesis 2. The availability of kin in households with more adult members will enable children to migrate. The number of adult sisters a son has is positively associated with the odds that he becomes a migrant. The number of brothers or sisters a daughter has is not related to her odds of labor migration. These results suggest a qualification to the expectation that the availability of kin represents a source of direct substitution of labor for migrant children. Direct substitution would require that one nonmigrant son's labor would replace the labor of his absent brother. Rather, daughters' availability may represent a labor supply reserve from which the family draws when other children are absent.

Hypothesis 3. Households where more children have been to the United States already will be more likely to send other adult children as migrants. The analysis presents strong support for this hypothesis, consistent with previous research (Palloni et al. 2001). Sons and daughters are more likely to migrate when a sibling or the household head has previously traveled to the United States, and family migration experience is associated with a greater likelihood of both labor and non-labor migration for daughters.

Hypothesis 4. Children will be more influenced by the migration behavior of their same-sex siblings than by that of their opposite-sex siblings. The odds that a child will become a migrant are higher when a same-sex sibling has migration experience. In particular, the odds that a daughter will become a labor migrant when a sister has preceded her to the United States are 60 percent higher for urban women and more than 100 percent higher for rural women, compared to the odds when a brother has been to the United States. Sons are more influenced by brothers' migration experience than by sisters', but in general, sons are less influenced by their siblings' behavior than are daughters.

Hypothesis 5. Children in urban areas will be more influenced by their siblings' migration experience and less influenced by the community-level migration experience, vis-à-vis adult children in rural areas. The comparison of the factors associated with rural and urban children's migration supports this hypothesis. Urban sons and daughters are more influenced by the migration experience of their siblings and less influenced by the level of experience in their community compared to rural sons and daughters. The mechanisms that explain this pattern were not explored, but may include the proximity, frequency, and variety of community ties in rural areas compared to urban areas.

Hypothesis 6. If economic need prevails as the motivator of children's migration, younger children in the parental household will be less likely to migrate if siblings precede them as migrants. But if social capital is the driving force behind children's migration, younger siblings will be more likely to go when other siblings have already migrated. Results support the hypothesis associated with economic need for sons, but the story for daughters appears to require a third interpretation. Indeed, not all children are equally likely to become migrants when siblings have preceded them. Higher birth order children (higher than third-born) are less likely to become migrants when a same-sex sibling has already been to the United States. For sons, this interaction suggests that the decision to migrate is motivated both by the availability of social capital and by economic need. If an older brother has already ventured to the United States, younger sons are less likely to convert their social capital into migration-specific resources if there are fewer younger siblings behind them.

Among daughters, younger children with sisters in the United States are less likely than others to become either labor or non-labor migrants. If the interaction were significant only in predicting labor migration, we might conclude that younger daughters were less likely to migrate because the parental household's economic need had diminished in response to older children's migration. But because the interaction also negatively predicts non-labor migration, an alternative explanation is required. Younger daughters may be expected to remain in the parental household to provide instrumental support when older siblings live in the United States, either because of traditional expectations or because nonmigrant daughters are valued by parents as a flexible labor supply source.

CHAPTER 5

Homeleaving by Nonmigrant Siblings

Mexico's rapid demographic change during the twentieth century had significant consequences for the composition and organization of households (DeVos 1995; Montes de Oca 1996). International migration by young adults is a component of demographic change that potentially influences the composition of the parental household in two ways: first, through the migrants' absence, which reduces the pool of kin available for coresidence with parents; and second, through the association that the migrant children's absence shares with the homeleaving patterns of nonmigrant siblings. The second cause is significant because children's international migration introduces a mechanism that interrupts patterns of home separation in Mexico traditionally associated with marriage and new family formation (De Vos 1989). The timing and context of the migration event are significant not only for the migrant, but for his siblings, whose own exits from and entries back into the household of origin may be influenced by the migrant's departure.

Using nonmigrant children in Mexico[31] as the unit of analysis, the objective of this chapter is to determine whether children's departure

---

[31] Children who remain in Mexico, or nonmigrant children, are those who had never migrated to the United States before interview. They may be internal migrants within Mexico.

from the parental household is associated with the U.S. migration behavior of one's siblings. The competing factors that influence children's homeleaving are conceptualized within the framework of the domestic life cycle approach developed by Gonzalez de la Rocha (1994). These factors include children's own life course transitions like marriage and labor force entry, the life cycle stage of the parental household, including family size, dependency, and head's work status, and the role of siblings' migration within the parental household.

The analysis is intended to identify the "ripple effects" of international migration on household organization in Mexico. Beyond that, it is intended to expand the literature on homeleaving by taking into account the behavior of other individuals to explain the decision to move out of the parents' home. Frequently, homeleaving is described as a function of a single individual's attributes combined with household-level characteristics. But homeleaving may be a decision made in reaction to or in tandem with the decisions of other adult children from the household. By controlling for the behavior of siblings, and by interacting measures of those behaviors with the attributes of nonmigrants, we can assess the extent to which the likelihood of homeleaving is influenced not only by one's own attributes and background, but by the life course transitions of kin.

THE CONTEXT OF HOMELEAVING IN MEXICO

In both urban and rural areas of Mexico, children's homeleaving represents a tension between children's desire to establish a nuclear household on the one hand, and parents' desire to receive economic gains from children's work on the other. Several studies conducted during the 1980's found that for working-class household heads in urban areas, the only way to improve economic standing is through the household. Over the course of a career, workers do not systematically receive wage increases, so quality of life does not necessarily improve with job tenure, assuming that a worker even remains with the same employer over a working lifetime. Instead, the better-off households are those that have more children of working age, more workers, a lower dependency ratio, and more migration (Selby, Murphy, and Lorenzen 1990). Economic crises like those experienced in Mexico in the early 1980's and early 1990's exacerbate the need for more workers per household in response to men's unemployment and underemployment (Gonzalez de la Rocha 1995). In rural areas as well, parents have an incentive to retain children as workers in the household: parental households with *ejido* landholdings use children's labor in order to maximize their comparative advantage of lower labor costs compared to private agriculture (deJanvry, Gordillo, and Sadoulet 1997). As a result, the heads of better-off households in both urban and rural areas are reluctant to lose household members to new family formation. Describing the urban household in Mexico, Selby, Murphy, and Lorenzen (1990) concluded that

> the most critical point in the domestic cycle in the city occurs when children leave school, establish themselves in some kind of occupation or more or less steady employment, and begin to wind down the courtship process in preparation for marriage. ...[I]t is critical at this point that the parents of the couple make arrangements to retain the couple's services in both the wage-earning and the domestic sphere (p. 59).

Despite the significance of this juncture for the economic well-being of the parental household, research has given little attention to the mechanisms associated with protracting or abbreviating the duration of its extension.

Gonzalez de la Rocha (1994) has described the household life cycle stages on either side of this juncture as the phases of consolidation and dispersion. The consolidated household is characterized by children's employment, male household heads' transition from physically demanding labor to less lucrative service work, and equilibrium between earnings and consumption in the household. Measurable attributes of the consolidated household include a low dependency ratio, larger household size, older average age among children, men's and women's labor force participation, and asset accumulation. Dispersion, on the other hand, is marked by children's moves to nuclear households, and parents are more likely to experience poverty and dependence on other kin.

Migration by some children might accelerate or delay the transition to a dispersed parental household, depending on what role migration plays in the household economy, and how other household members behave in the presence of migration. Gonzalez de la Rocha (2001) hypothesized that migration would accelerate the dispersion of the urban household during a period of macroeconomic crisis because parents would lose an immediate source of labor and income. But nonmigrant children may remain in the parents' household in Mexico in order to consolidate resources during the economically stressful period when the migrant is becoming established abroad or to replace their siblings as caregivers and economic providers to parents. Alternatively, adult children's sustained migration may be indicative of an advanced life cycle stage in the household, with other children departing for more traditional reasons like marriage and entry into the domestic labor force, independent of migration events. Table 5.1 summarizes the potential associations between children's international migration and nonmigrant siblings' own homeleaving.

These hypotheses about the direction of an association should be considered in the context of the various models of the household economy elaborated in chapter 2. The household as moral economy approach assumes that household members act on common interests and pool resources in order to maximize the joint utility function of the household. Under that framework, some children would migrate and others would move out of the parental household only if such choices improved the standing of the household, or at least did not compromise the household's standing. In that case, children's migration would serve the joint utility of the household only if other productive household members remain in the household longer than they would otherwise; that is, if children's migration delays homeleaving by other children. If migration accelerates the dispersion of the parental household, or if nonmigrant children appear to depart from the household independent of their siblings' behavior, the findings would suggest that the household as moral economy approach is inadequate for understanding how children's migration affects parental households in Mexico, and the household strategies model or the household bargaining model may be more appropriate.

Table 5.1 Potential associations between children's international migration and nonmigrant siblings homeleaving

Direction of association	Pattern of homeleaving by nonmigrants
Children's migration *delays* homeleaving by other children	Nonmigrant children remain in parental household despite passing through life course stages that typically are associated with homeleaving
Children's migration *accelerates* dispersion of parental household	Nonmigrants with migrant siblings more likely to live outside parents' home compared to nonmigrants without migrant siblings
Children's migration is associated with the natural dispersion of the parental household, but *does not cause* the dispersion	Older nonmigrant children and married children are more likely to live outside the parental household than are their younger, unmarried siblings

THE EFFECTS OF INTERNATIONAL MIGRATION ON HOUSEHOLDS IN MEXICO

Although Mexican women have joined migration streams in significant numbers in the past 20 years, the majority of international migrants, and especially temporary migrants, are men. The consequences of this pattern are apparent in Mexico's age and sex structure for the year 2000.[32] Since 1980, the resident Mexican population has included more women than men, and the distribution is projected to remain skewed into the foreseeable future. This phenomenon is not a function of mortality differentials alone. Figure 5.1 shows the age and sex structure of Mexico in 2000. The bars indicate that although males outnumber females before age 20, there are more women than men in all other 5-year age groups in the adult population. The sex ratio drops precipitously after age 14, plateaus around age 30, and begins to drop again as a result of mortality differentials around age 55. This pattern is consistent with the finding that most labor migrants are young adults who return to Mexico permanently after the pressures of early family formation have eased (Massey, Alarcon, Durand, and Gonzalez 1987).

The observed reversal in sex ratios in adulthood is not unusual for the region. The same pattern holds in Latin America as a whole (Figure 5.2). However, the decline is much sharper among young adults, and the plateau that is observed in Mexico in middle adulthood is not apparent for the entire region. These distinct patterns reflect that although Mexico is not unique among Latin American countries for sending migrants to the United States, the flow of migrants from Mexico, in absolute and relative terms, far exceeds migrant outflows from elsewhere in the region.

The sex and age composition of migrant flows has important consequences for individuals with migrant kin who remain in Mexico themselves. In the presence of migration, sex- and age-based role expectations within Mexico change in order to accommodate the loss of local labor. Distinctive migration patterns also change nuptiality patterns by limiting the availability of men or women in the local marriage market, and change fertility patterns (although not total marital fertility) by limiting the time couples are together (Lindstrom and Saucedo 2002). These social and demographic responses to

---

[32] CELADE 1998 estimates.

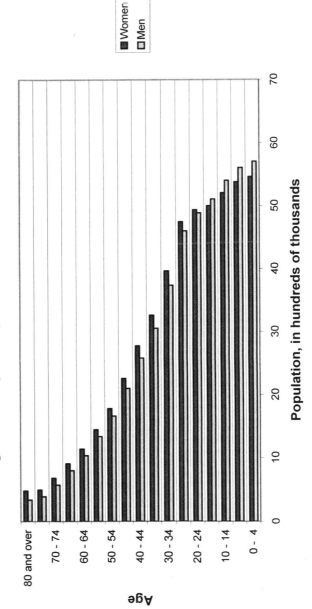

Figure 5.1: Projected age distribution in Mexico, 2000

Women
Men

Age

Population, in hundreds of thousands

Source: CELADE 1998

99

Figure 5.2: Sex ratio in Mexico and Latin America, 2000

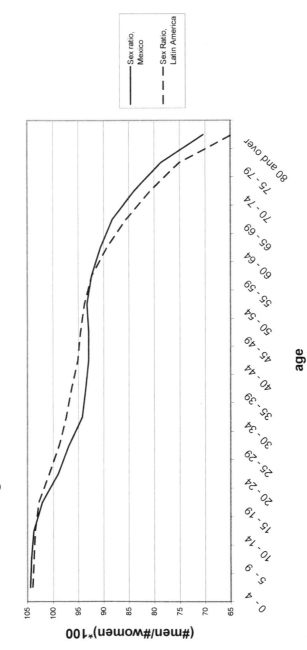

Source: CELADE 1998

100

migration potentially affect how long children remain in their parents' homes, either taking on new roles, waiting for marriage, or raising young children. From the perspective of the domestic life cycle framework, such changes would extend the consolidation phase of the parental household.

Changes in population distribution imply concomitant changes in intergenerational relations. These changes include differences in coresidence patterns as well as in the allocation of exchanges of time and resources between parents and children. In Mexico, average household size has declined from 5.2 to 4.8 members since 1970, but extended households increased from 19.6 to 24.5 percent of all non-solitary households. These contrasting changes result from simultaneous demographic processes. Household size has declined because of lower fertility rates and out-migration. At the same time, coresidence has become more prevalent due to several factors, including aging parents' economic need in the absence of adequate social security programs, married children's continued presence in the household, and the incorporation of migrant relatives who cannot maintain a separate household in Mexico (Flores and Gomez 1997).

Sociological research on the relationship between demographic processes and the living arrangements of adult children emphasizes the effects of fertility, mortality, and nuptiality. The effect of migration on living arrangements has been less studied. The existing literature focuses on the individual characteristics associated with children leaving and returning to the parents' home (DaVanzo and Goldscheider 1990; Goldscheider and Goldscheider 1993), the competing risks of labor force participation and marriage as pathways to home-leaving (DeVos 1989; Goldscheider and Goldscheider 1993), and the characteristics of family members that motivate parents to move closer to some children rather than to others (Clark and Wolf 1992; Litwak and Longino 1987).

But research on elderly living arrangements in Mexico indicates that children's international migration does influence the composition of the parental household (Kanaiaupuni 1999). Elderly parents with married U.S. migrant children are substantially more likely to live alone, although the effect of having at least one unmarried child with migration experience who is locally available increases the parents' chance of coresidence with children. However, not all U.S. migration is associated with living arrangements in the parental households. The effect of unmarried children's migration on living arrangements was insignificant, while the migration of married children increased the odds of parents living alone. These findings suggest that migration by some children puts pressure on those who remain to reconsider their choices about homeleaving, or perhaps, to return to the parental home when siblings leave Mexico for long spells. However, these effects might not hold for adult children from parental households with younger heads.

The current research considers how one child's transition out of the household through migration affects the remaining children, rather than the parents. In terms of the domestic life cycle framework, how might the composition and quality of U.S. migration affect young adult children's homeleaving decisions in Mexico? First, in the aggregate, as figure 5.2 indicates, the life course stage under consideration (age 16-25) stands at the beginning of a marked decline in Mexico's sex ratio, a decline potentially explained by men's out-migration. At the household level, sisters and parents might use coresidence as a response to this change. Second, children's migration may influence expectations about providing care to parents through money, physical assistance, or household labor. If sons who previously would have stayed in the parental household after marriage migrate instead, their parents may gain a source of remittances, but they will lose a source of labor and local economic support. Nonmigrant children may step in to fill this role. On the other hand, migrant children may leave their spouses and children in the parents' care. This extended household arrangement may allow other children to leave for work within Mexico, if the new members of the household take on responsibilities of maintaining the parental household.

The current chapter assesses how much of nonmigrants' homeleaving decisions are directly associated with the household attachment of migrant siblings, compared to the importance of the availability of other kin, the life cycle stage of the household, and individual life course transitions like marriage. *Availability of kin* indicates the supply of potential coresidents. Within the domestic life cycle framework, the availability of kin, and especially the availability of adult children, reflects where the household stands between the phases of consolidation and dispersion. Prior research has found that as the number of adult children a parent has increases, the odds of living with at least one child also increase (Martin and Kinsella 1994; Wolf 1994; Wolf and Soldo 1988). This pattern holds among elderly parents in Mexico as well (Kanaiaupuni 1999). From the perspective of children, however, research outside Mexico has found that as the number of siblings increases, children leave at home at younger ages (see White 1994).

The *economic and physical needs* of family members also determine whether children remain in the household. From this perspective, the *demand* for care or support, rather than the supply, influences coresidence. If parents of adult children are healthy and financially independent, children will experience fewer demands to remain in the household (Blank 1998). However, as economic and physical well-being decline, parents will turn to their children for support (Mutchler and Burr 1991). Literature in this area focuses on widows, who have fewer economic resources than spouses because they have less labor force experience (Boyd 1989; Burr and Mutchler 1993).

Parents' poor health and economic need do not necessarily predict that children will remain in or return to the parents' home intending to provide care. Most literature on delays to homeleaving or returns to the parents' home highlights the instability of a child's early years in adulthood. Children are likely to return to the parents' household because of their own financial insecurity (DaVanzo and Goldscheider 1990). When parents are in need of support, they typically enter the child's home, rather than ask children to relocate (Wolf 1994). Although these findings are useful for identifying motives to coreside from the child's perspective as well as the parents', this research has not been extended to Mexico, and the findings are not necessarily generalizable to that population.

In Mexico, urban residence predicts parent/adult child coresidence (Solis 1999). This finding is interpreted as a reflection of the higher cost of living relative to rural areas, and, consequently, as a measure of economic strain. Coresidence in urban areas also points to the benefits of the extended household as a productive unit where homework (assembly work that requires little mechanization) is part of the local industrial chain (Gonzalez de la Rocha 1994). The finding that families often coreside in urban areas also appears in the literature on living arrangements in Malaysia (Chan and DaVanzo 1994) and in developing countries generally (Martin and Kinsella 1994). Using data from the 1994 Sociodemographic Survey on Aging in Mexico, Solís (1999) also finds that home ownership by the elderly person (a common measure of socioeconomic status in the sociological literature on Mexico) negatively predicts coresidence with children.

Individual life course transitions also explain adult children's coresidence. Historically, marriage has been the most powerful indicator of the timing of homeleaving, but in recent decades, homeleaving has occurred in conjunction with entry into college or the labor force, or as a result of disruptions to family structure (DaVanzo and Goldscheider 1990; Goldscheider and Goldscheider 1993; White 1994). Within Mexico, empirical research supports the argument that children's marriage and labor force entry are the life course transitions most likely to disrupt the form of the parental household, at least in urban areas. But nonmigrant sons and daughters will experience these transitions differently, because work and marriage have different meanings for men and women. For men, entry into the labor force denotes the beginning of adulthood and a lifetime of paid employment. Although sons contribute earnings to the parental household, they are encouraged to keep part of their earnings for their own expenses, and mother and sisters "repay" the laboring son with meals and clean clothing (Gonzalez de la Rocha 1994). For women, often the period between the end of school and the entry to marriage represents the only opportunity to engage in full-time work in the formal sector and to be treated as a significant contributor to the household. The experience of work, however, does not give daughters the autonomy that sons experience. They have less discretion with their earnings, and parents and siblings closely guard women's behavior outside the home and workplace (Gonzalez de la Rocha 1994).

Marriage also has different consequences for sons and daughters. Daughters typically leave the parental home and move in with parents-in-law, while married sons remain with parents until the first children are born and the need for space and privacy overwhelms the benefits of a shared household economy (Selby, Murphy, and Lorenzen 1990). For daughters, then, marriage represents a transition out of the labor force and the move to another household, where her interests may be subordinate both to her husband's and to those of other household members, including her mother-in-law. A recently married woman may receive an allowance from her husband, but may not know his actual earnings or how they are spent. Therefore, the likelihood that she would continue to contribute to her own parental household after marriage is small. With some children already gone as migrants, parents might encourage a nonmigrant daughter to delay marriage in order to continue benefiting from her waged labor, or might support a new household form, in which the married daughter would remain in the household, and her new husband would contribute to the household economy. Married sons, on the other hand, might be encouraged to extend their stay so that parents may continue to receive the benefits of an extended household.

DATA AND METHODS

The analysis uses the 89 communities from the Mexican Migration Project that were considered in the preceding chapter. In the current analysis, the sample is limited to include only adult children with no migration experience who are between age 16 and age 25 in the interview year. Age 25 is used as a cutoff in order to focus on the likelihood of homeleaving in early adulthood only. The resulting sample includes 12,081 children from 5,086 households.

The analysis begins by comparing nonmigrant children living in the parental household to those living elsewhere to assess how much of the observed difference in living arrangements results from characteristics of the children, their parental households, and siblings' migration behavior. Multivariate logistic regression models estimate the log-likelihood that a nonmigrant child lives outside the parental household as a function of a.) the nonmigrant child's individual characteristics, including age, marital status, sex, and education; b.) the availability of other kin for coresidence, measured as the number of adult siblings the nonmigrant child has; c.) the parental household's economic resources; and d.) the prevalence of migration among siblings.

Models are presented separately for rural and urban households. Macroeconomic and demographic contexts in rural and urban areas are sufficiently different that the motives and timing for migration and for homeleaving are potentially distinctive. For example, children in rural households are more likely than urban households to leave the parental household to reside elsewhere in Mexico; urban children typically remain in school longer than rural children, and may delay other life course transitions as a result; and rural and urban children may be subject to different regimes for the timing of marriage, particularly if significant out-migration by young rural men reduces the size of the local marriage market.

Hypotheses

The analysis considers the relationship between adult children's migration and the homeleaving behavior of adult nonmigrant siblings in the context of the three possible associations described in table 5.1. If children's migration accelerates the dispersion of the parental household, nonmigrant children will be more likely to live outside the parental household even when they are not yet married or, for sons, when they are not in the labor force. If, in contrast, children's migration delays the dispersion of the parental household, married nonmigrant children and working sons will be more likely to remain in the parental household when they have migrant siblings. Finally, if children's migration and the departure of nonmigrant children from the parental household co-occur because the parental household has aged into a more advanced life course stage rather than because they are causally connected, nonmigrant children's living arrangements will be predicted by their own marital and employment status, rather than by siblings' behavior.

Independent variables

The regression equation includes the following covariates:

Age of the adult child: The probability of homeleaving is expected to increase with age. The measure of age is lagged by one year.

Years of education: Education is expected to have a positive relationship with home separation because more education should allow children to pursue better-paying jobs and to establish a separate household.

Sex: All else equal, sons are expected to remain in their parents' household longer than daughters, who marry and leave the home at younger ages.

Marital status: Marriage is expected to strongly predict home separation, but more strongly for daughters than for sons.

Birth order: Traditionally, younger children have helped to maintain the parental household as older siblings have departed, with the youngest child remaining in the household. If migration has disrupted that pattern, higher birth order children in a family may be expected to take on the role of caregiver to aging parents. The probability of living outside the home is expected to decrease as birth order increases.

Number of adult children in the family: The number of children age 15 or over represents the kin available to the household for coresidence.

Work status of household head: Adult children of household heads who are out of the labor force, due either to retirement or unemployment, are expected to remain in the parents' household in order to provide an additional source of income.

Household head's migration status: Adult children with one parent in the United States are expected to remain in the resident parent's household in order to provide a source of immediate income.

Dependency ratio: The number of non-working household members to the number of workers represents the household's dependency ratio. Dependents include minors, the elderly and anyone who is not counted as employed on the household roster. To the extent that women's occasional or informal labor is not counted as "paid work" by the household head, the dependency ratio may be overestimated.

Household wealth: A socioeconomic index scored 0 to 3 measures whether the household head owns the household's residence (1) or not (0); whether the household head owns a business (1) or not (0); and whether the household owns at least 5 hectares of land (Donato and Kanaiaupuni 2000). A higher SES index is expected to negatively predict children's homeleaving, because children will remain to take advantage of assets, all else equal. This indicator is lagged by one year.[33]

Period of interview: Interviews were conducted between 1987 and 2002. A dummy variable indicates whether a nonmigrant child's parent was interviewed between 1987 and 1992 or later.

DESCRIPTIVE RESULTS

Table 5.2 compares adult children living apart from parents to those who coreside. Asterisks indicate significant differences between the two groups at p<.05. About a quarter of nonmigrant children age 16 to 25 live in separate households from their parents. The descriptive data show significant differences between the two groups in the number of active migrant siblings a child has. Children who live outside the

---

[33] Donato and Kanaiaupuni's (2000) measure also indicates whether the household's residence had a tile floor and at least five rooms. These data are available for the residence in the year of interview, but they are not available for residences owned in earlier years. The SES measure used in the current analysis excludes those indicators of housing quality in order to make the measure analogous to the measure used in the retrospective analysis in the preceding chapter.

Table 5.2 Characteristics of nonmigrant children by household membership status, unweighted means and frequencies, MMP93

	Living in Parental Household		Living Outside Parental Household		
	Mean	SD	Mean		SD
Child's characteristics					
Age	18.818	2.980	21.717	*	2.590
Years of education	8.629	3.302	8.066	*	3.557
Male	0.487		0.353	*	
Never married	0.941		0.184	*	
Married	0.056		0.813	*	
Formerly married	0.003		0.004		
Employed	0.419		0.424		
Birth order	3.946	2.741	4.014		2.642
Number of brothers in the U.S.	0.271	0.758	0.345	*	0.847
Number of sisters in the U.S.	0.089	0.417	0.133	*	0.486
Household characteristics					
Rural residence	0.205		0.218		
Head is employed	0.941		0.905	*	
Socioeconomic status index (0-3)	1.075	0.695	1.084		0.682
Number of adult sons	2.098	1.627	2.069		1.542
Number of adult daughters	2.088	1.654	2.377	*	1.614
Dependency ratio in parental household	2.015	1.776	1.747	*	1.524
Head is in U.S.	0.076		0.058	*	
Interview period					
1987-1992	0.397		0.368	*	
1993-2000	0.604		0.632	*	
N	8969		3112		

*Group differences are statistically significant at $p < .05$

parental household have more migrant brothers and sisters. On average, a nonmigrant child living outside the parental household has .345 brothers in the United States and .133 migrant sisters. A child living in the parental household has .271 migrant brothers and .089 migrant sisters. The group differences are significant at the .05 level. In the context of the domestic life cycle framework, the comparison suggests that migration by some children appears to be associated with the general dispersion of the parental household, rather than with protracted consolidation by nonmigrant siblings.

In the descriptive summary, it is unclear to what extent siblings' migration is associated with nonmigrant children's homeleaving once children's marital status and employment status are taken into account. Adult children in separate households share several characteristics positively associated with homeleaving. They are slightly older and more often married, and come from larger families with more adult daughters and a lower dependency ratio. They are not more likely to work, however. This apparent lack of difference reflects variation by gender in labor force participation. Sons continue to work after they leave home and establish a separate household, but daughters' labor force participation typically ends after marriage.

The distinctions in age, marital and employment status, and dependency ratios lend support to the hypothesis that children's homeleaving and siblings' migration appear to be related only because the parental household is reaching an advanced life course stage and children's moves correspond to the their own life course transitions. The more detailed, multivariate analysis that follows permits a test of the alternative hypothesis, that in the presence of siblings' migration, some nonmigrant children remain in the parental household despite passing through life course stages that typically are associated with homeleaving.

MULTIVARIATE RESULTS

The results from logistic regressions presented in table 5.3 are estimates of the odds of an adult child living outside the parental household compared to living in that household.[34] The odds are predicted as a

---

[34] Note that the marital status category "formerly married" is excluded for the model for rural sons. There were no rural sons in the sample who had been formerly married.

Table 5.3 Logistic regressions predicting whether nonmigrants live outside parental household, by sex and urban residence, MMP93

	Rural Men		Urban Men	
	OR	SE	OR	SE
Child's characteristics				
Age	1.204	0.056**	1.242	0.033**
Years of education	1.025	0.044	1.087	0.024**
Married	14.415	5.134**	38.386	6.667**
Formerly married			1.769	2.176
Employed	1.486	0.472	2.497	0.502**
Birth order	1.064	0.136	1.03	0.079
Number of brothers in the U.S.	0.804	0.176	0.992	0.166
Number of sisters in the U.S.	0.764	0.199	1.378	0.220*
Brothers in U.S.*married	0.988	0.292	0.842	0.181

Table 5.3 Logistic regressions predicting whether nonmigrants live outside parental household, by sex and urban residence, MMP93, continued

	Rural Men		Urban Men	
	OR	SE	OR	SE
Household characteristics				
Head is employed	1.149	0.667	0.968	0.253
Socioeconomic status index (0-3)	0.97	0.188	0.725	0.083**
Number of adult sons	0.987	0.15	1.012	0.095
Number of adult daughters	0.863	0.132	0.991	0.089
Dependency ratio in parental household	0.789	0.114	0.661	0.080**
Dependency ratio*working	2.001	0.362	2.594	0.375**
Head is in U.S.	0.729	0.415	0.737	0.283
Interview period				
1993-2002 (vs. 1987-1992)	2.046	0.538**	0.733	0.114*
Observations	1073		4390	

Table 5.3 Logistic regressions predicting whether nonmigrants live outside parental household, by sex and urban residence. MMP93, continued

	Rural Women		Urban Women	
	OR	SE	OR	SE
Child's characteristics				
Age	1.102	0.044*	1.128	0.028**
Years of education	1.053	0.054	1.025	0.023
Married	98.172	34.516**	126.001	20.120**
Formerly married	8.446	6.976**	9.4	5.550**
Employed	3.074	0.888**	1.17	0.252
Birth order	1.115	0.125	0.975	0.06
Number of brothers in the U.S.	0.929	0.145	0.939	0.097
Number of sisters in the U.S.	0.494	0.170*	1.601	0.292**
Sisters in U.S.*married	3.432	2.220+	0.635	0.146*

112

Table 5.3 Logistic regressions predicting whether nonmigrants live outside parental household, by sex and urban residence, MMP93, continued

	Rural Women		Urban Women	
	OR	SE	OR	SE
Household characteristics				
Head is employed	1.687	0.537	0.98	0.337
Socioeconomic status index (0-3)	0.813	0.137	1.022	0.129
Number of adult sons	1.029	0.134	0.984	0.081
Number of adult daughters	0.933	0.132	1.146	0.091+
Dependency ratio in parental household	0.908	0.087	0.879	0.040**
Dependency ratio*working	2.396	0.407**	1.728	0.249**
Head is in U.S.	0.822	0.225	1.106	0.291
Interview period				
1993-2002 (vs. 1987-1992)	2.256	0.591**	0.951	0.147
Observations	1443		5175	

+ significant at 10%; * significant at 5%; ** significant at 1%

113

function of the child's own human capital characteristics and marital status, the number of adult and minor siblings available to coreside with the parents, economic need in the parents' household, and migration prevalence in the family. Separate models are estimated for sons and daughters in urban and rural communities.

The results indicate that individual life course transitions are the strongest predictors of children's residential arrangements. For all groups, child's age and being currently married have strong positive effects on the odds of living apart from parents. However, the effect of being married is much stronger for women and urban residents than for men and rural residents. The odds that a married urban woman will live outside the parental household are about 125 to 1, compared to odds of only 13 to 1 for a married rural man.

For urban sons and for rural daughters, being employed is also associated with living outside the parental household. Because daughters' departure from the household is typically associated with marriage rather than with labor force participation, the significance of employment for rural daughters initially seems counterintuitive. One plausible explanation is that historically women more often than men have migrated temporarily within Mexico (although internal migration has become more masculinized in recent years), and much of that migration is from rural to urban areas. Hence, rural daughters more so than urban daughters or rural men may be likely to depart the parental household to work elsewhere, but their absence may be only temporary.

Individual life course transitions explain much of the variation in children's residence decisions, but siblings' migration also plays a part. However, that part is strongly associated with gender, and is inconsistent in its effects. Sisters' migration is associated with nonmigrant children's residence choices, but more so for daughters than for sons. In rural areas, the odds of living outside the parental household are .491 for women with a sister in the United States, indicating that sisters' migration is associated with adult daughters remaining in the parental household. In contrast, for daughters in urban areas, the odds ratio for living elsewhere is 1.597 when there is a sister in the United States, meaning that sisters' migration is associated with nonmigrant daughters' departure from the parental household.

The models predicting daughters' residence include an interaction term for the number of sisters in the United States and a nonmigrant daughter's marital status. The expectation is that sisters' migration has different ramifications for a nonmigrant daughter's choice about whether to live in the parental household if the nonmigrant daughter is married or unmarried. A model that includes an interaction term requires particular attention to its interpretation. The "main effect" of migration is represented by the odds ratio associated with the number of sisters in the United States (as described above). The interaction effect is the combination of three components: the main effect of being married, the main effect of the number of sisters in the United States, and the interaction term between being married and the number of sisters abroad.

For married daughters from rural areas, the statistically significant interaction term shows that there is a uniquely positive effect of having a sister in the United States on the odds of living outside the parental household. The odds of living outside the parental household are 3.679 times higher for a married daughter with a sister abroad compared to daughters who are not married or who do not have migrant sister. For married daughters from urban areas, the interaction term shows that there is a uniquely *negative* effect of sisters' migration. The odds of living outside the parental household are slightly more than one-third smaller $((1-.638)*100=36.2\%)$ for married urban daughters with a migrant sister, compared to unmarried urban daughters or those without a migrant sibling.

The interpretation is different for unmarried daughters. Because they have a value of "0" on the "married" variable, they also have a value of "0" on the interaction term (married*number of sisters in the United States). Therefore, for unmarried daughters, the main effect of the number of sisters in the United States is the *total* effect of sisters' migration on the odds of residing outside the parental household. For unmarried rural daughters, the odds of living outside the parental household are reduced by half when a sister is in the United States $((1-.491)*100=50.9\%)$, compared to when no sisters are abroad; for unmarried urban daughters, the odds of living outside increase by about 60 percent when a sister is in the United States.

For nonmigrant urban sons, sisters' migration has a positive, direct effect on living outside the parental household. The effect is smaller in magnitude and statistical significance compared to the results for urban daughters, but the interpretation is the same: sisters' migration appears to be associated with the accelerated dispersion of the urban household. For nonmigrant rural sons, siblings' migration has no statistically significant effect.

The relevant interaction in the models of nonmigrant sons' residence is between the son's marital status and the number of brothers in the United States, rather than the number of sisters. The nonsignificant interaction term indicates that there is no unique effect of brothers' migration for married sons compared to unmarried sons.[35]

To assess the relationship between the household's dependency ratio and individual children's economic contributions, the analysis includes an interaction between work status and the household dependency ratio. The dependency ratio is centered at its mean. The odds represent the effect of a one-unit change above or below the mean of the dependency ratio. The interaction term represents the effect of working when the parental household's dependency ratio is above or below the mean level. Parallel to the interpretation of interaction effects described above, the "main effect" of the dependency ratio represents its total effect for children who are not working. For children who do work, the total effect is the combination of the main effects of working and of the dependency ratio as well as the interaction effect.

The results indicate that where the dependency ratio is higher than average, adult children who are not employed are less likely to live outside the household compared to where there are fewer dependents per worker. However, when an adult child is working and the dependency ratio is above average, he is more likely to live outside the household, rather than to remain in the household to contribute earnings directly.

Table 5.4 summarizes the results in terms of average probabilities based on the results presented in table 5.3. All independent variables are held at the mean except the variables of interest in each cell. The probability of living in a separate household is presented for rural and urban sons and daughters. For each type of adult child, two factors vary: marital status and the presence of a sister in the United States. The probability that an unmarried son from a rural household will live in a separate household when he has a sister in the United States is .08, compared to a probability of .10 for an identical son with no migrant

---

[35] Models with an interaction between work status and siblings' migration were also tested to assess whether nonmigrant children behave differently in the presence of siblings' migration when they are employed compared to when they are not employed. The interaction terms were insignificant across the board, and the models are not presented here.

Table 5.4. Probability that a nonmigrant child resides outside the parental household, by marital status, urbanicity, and presence of siblings in the United States, MMP93

		No siblings in the United States	One sister in the United States
Nonmigrant child is never married	Rural Sons	0.10	0.08
	Urban sons	0.05	0.06
	Rural Daughters	0.10	0.05
	Urban Daughters	0.04	0.06
Nonmigrant child is married	Rural Sons	0.61	0.54
	Urban sons	0.65	0.72
	Rural Daughters	0.91	0.95
	Urban Daughters	0.83	0.83

sisters. In other words, the probability that an unmarried rural son will live outside the parental household is reduced by 20 percent when he has a migrant sister, compared to when he has no siblings in the United States. A married rural son is about 11 percent less likely to live outside the parental home when he has a migrant sister compared to a similar son without migrant siblings $(1-(.54/.61)=.115)$. For urban sons, the change in the magnitude of the probabilities is reversed: urban sons with one migrant sister are somewhat *more* likely to live outside the parental household compared to urban sons without migrant sisters.

Among daughters, the influence of sisters' migration on the probability of living outside the parental household is stronger in rural communities. Unmarried daughters from rural households have a probability of living outside the parental household of only .05 when a sister is in the United States. The probability of living outside is twice as high, or .10, for unmarried sisters without a migrant sibling. For married daughters from rural households, the effect of sisters' migration on the probability of living outside works in the opposite direction: married daughters are more likely to live outside when they have a migrant sister compared to when they do not. But the real effect of sisters' migration for married daughters is negligible in real terms: without a migrant sibling, the probability is .91, and with a migrant sister, it is .95. In qualitative terms, this represents a change in the likelihood of living outside the household from a near certainty to a very near certainty. For urban daughters, the effect of sisters' migration on the probability of living outside the parental household is small. For unmarried daughters, the direction of the effect of sisters' migration is opposite that for rural unmarried daughters. Urban unmarried daughters with a sister in the United States are fifty percent more likely to reside outside the parental household, although the absolute change in probabilities is small, changing to .06 from .04 when a sister is abroad. For married daughters, sisters' migration makes no difference in the probability of living outside the parental household because the effect of marital status overwhelms the other attributes accounted for in the model.

DISCUSSION

It is important to recall that the data employed in this research lack information about the timing of homeleaving for nonmigrants. As a result, we cannot establish the temporal ordering of nonmigrants' homeleaving and siblings' migration. The results and interpretation presented here describe an association consistent with the domestic life cycle model of household organization in Mexico, but do not represent a dynamic process. Research on migration and households would be well-served by data that enable the analysis of family dynamics and the timing of individual life course events together.

The objective of this chapter was to determine whether children's departure from the parental household is associated with the U.S. migration behavior of one's siblings. To understand how migration and homeleaving events among siblings might be associated, the analysis built on the domestic life cycle framework described by Gonzalez de la Rocha (1994) and assessed the validity of three competing hypotheses: If children's migration were to accelerate the dispersion of the parental household, nonmigrant children would be more likely to live outside the parental household even when they are not yet married or, for sons, when they are not in the labor force. If, in contrast, children's migration were to delay the dispersion of the parental household, married nonmigrant children and working sons would be more likely to remain in the parental household when they have migrant siblings. And if children's migration and the departure of nonmigrant children from the parental household were to co-occur because the parental household has aged into a more advanced life course stage rather than because they were causally connected, nonmigrant children's living arrangements would be predicted by their own marital and employment status, rather than by siblings' behavior.

The analysis does not show support for a single hypothesis. Rather, the association between homeleaving and siblings' migration is dependent on social context and on the sex of the children involved. Sisters' migration is associated with the homeleaving behavior of nonmigrant daughters in urban and rural areas and sons in urban areas, but not the behavior of sons in rural areas. Brothers' migration is unrelated to homeleaving by nonmigrant siblings.

In urban settings, sisters' migration is associated with the greater likelihood that nonmigrant daughters and sons will live outside the parental household. This association supports the hypothesis that children's migration accelerates the dispersion of the parental household in urban areas, as Gonzalez de la Rocha (2001) anticipated. In the statistical analysis, married daughters with sisters in the United States are marginally more likely to remain in the parental household than other daughters, but the effect is small compared to the magnitude of the effect of marriage on homeleaving. As a result, there is little support for the hypothesis that children's migration delays the dispersion of the household.

Among daughters in rural areas, the results of the statistical analysis are just the opposite of the results from urban areas. The results do not support the hypothesis that children's migration causes the accelerated dispersion of the parental household. Rather, daughters with sisters in the United States are more likely to remain in the parental household compared to daughters without migrant sisters. The interaction effect included in the model indicates that married daughters are marginally more likely to live outside the parental household when they have sisters in the United States, but the real impact of that association is relatively small. Overall, the analysis rejects the hypothesis of accelerated dispersion for daughters in rural areas.

This finding may indicate that in households where some daughters migrate internationally, other daughters who otherwise might have sought work elsewhere in Mexico instead remain in the parental household. Under that interpretation, the parental household might not be retaining more members than it would in the absence of children's international migration. Rather, there might be a swapping-out of children who depart. The children who would have become migrants within Mexico remain when their siblings travel to the United States; conversely, those international migrants might have remained in the household had their siblings traveled within Mexico. Such an arrangement would indicate that children's migration influences the composition, but not the size, of the parental household.

For nonmigrant sons in rural areas, siblings' migration is unrelated to homeleaving decisions. The analysis supports the third hypothesis, that children's homeleaving and siblings' migration co-occur not because of any causal link, but because the parental household has reached an advanced life course stage. Why is nonmigrant rural sons' behavior apparently impervious to the migration of siblings? Perhaps it is because rural sons are the most enmeshed in culture of migration. Historically, international migration has been male-dominated and rural in origin. As the analysis in chapter 3 indicated, children in rural areas are more strongly influenced to migrate themselves by the level of migration in the community and less by the behavior of their siblings compared to children in urban areas. For households with rural sons, international migration may be so normative that the household requires no adaptation to absorb the impact of migration.

For all of the nonmigrant children, homeleaving is explained largely by individual characteristics, including marital status and employment status, and by parental household attributes like the dependency ratio. Children, and especially daughters, who are married are much more likely than unmarried nonmigrant siblings to live in separate households. Working urban sons and rural daughters also are more likely to live outside the parental household. The significance of these life course markers is consistent with the causes of dispersion in the household life cycle model. Taking siblings' migration behavior into account does not significantly mediate individual or household attributes, but does add explanatory power to the multivariate model.

Returning to the various models of the household economy described in chapter 2, it would be overreaching to conclude that one model is best supported by the preceding analysis, because we do not directly observe the economic implications of children's homeleaving for the parental household, and so cannot determine whether children's homeleaving is detrimental. However, the analysis does offer some conclusions about how decisionmaking occurs in the parental household, which has implications for economic organization.

All nonmigrant children are more likely to live outside the parental household when they are employed and when the household dependency ratio is above average. In rural households, this might indicate that working children have moved to urban areas to work and remit earnings to the household, which would be consistent with the model of the household as a moral economy. In urban households, residing outside the parental household appears less consistent with boosting household income, if descriptions of the urban household economy (Selby, Murphy, and Lorenzen 1990, Gonzalez de la Rocha 1994) are accurate. Rather, homeleaving by working children in urban areas would diminish income in the parental household. Such an outcome would suggest that children and parents are in conflict about optimizing the parental household and would call for a perspective on the urban parental household derived from the household bargaining framework.

The effects of siblings' migration in rural and urban areas suggest a similar interpretation. In rural areas, unmarried daughters are more likely to remain in the parental household and married daughters are only slightly more likely to depart when they have a sister in the United States. As a result, children's migration may not be associated with a significant change in the economic organization of the parental household, suggesting that children are acting in concert to maintain the household economy. In urban areas, in contrast, siblings' migration is associated with the departure of nonmigrant sons and unmarried daughters, suggesting that migration is symptomatic of the dissolution of the household and children's independent decisionmaking.

CHAPTER 6

The Role of Migration in Cash
Transfers from Children to Parents

Remittances are Mexico's second-largest source of foreign revenue after oil, and the volume of transfers increases every year. Migrants working in the United States sent an estimated $4.2 billion to families in Mexico in 1996 (Latapi, Martin, Castro, and Donato 1998); estimated transfers in 2003 were $13 billion (Federal Reserve Bank of Dallas 2004), representing a three-fold increase in seven years. Typically, recipients put remittances toward consumption, including housing, food, and education, and toward investments in land, agriculture, and small businesses (Durand, Parrado, and Massey 1996). Although the merit of remittances as a source of income and revenue is debated (Jones 1998; Taylor, Arango, Hugo, Kouaouci, Massey, and Pellegrino 1996), empirical evidence indicates that remittances to Mexico are associated with rising standards of living and economic growth in migrant-sending communities (Adelman and Taylor 1990; Kanaiaupuni and Donato 1999; Stark and Lucas 1988; Taylor et al. 1996).

This chapter considers whether parents with adult migrant children receive cash transfers from children, and whether those contributions exceed contributions from parents with only nonmigrant children. The analysis considers the attributes of migrants, members of the parental household, and the household itself to determine what influences the frequency and size of transfers. Linked data from the Mexican Migration Project (MMP) (1994 and 1995) and from the 1996 Health and Migration Survey (HMS) on household migration prevalence and all sources of income in the preceding month are used to establish a relationship between children's migration and parents' cash transfer receipt.

In the migration literature, the transfer of remittances between children and their parents has received less attention than have transfers between husbands and wives (but see Wong, Soldo, and Capoferro 2000). Several reasons account for the emphasis on transfers in the household of procreation. First, where men migrate as husbands, their absence from the home may indicate an economically stressful period that precedes or results from their migration. Consequently, remittances may satisfy an urgent need for income. Second, studying the pattern of remittance transfers between husbands and wives provides material to test theories in various areas of household-based migration research, including split-household strategies, power dynamics between spouses, investment priorities, and the competing effects of parents' migration and earnings on children's well-being. Third, tracking the transfer of remittances from husband to wife may be easier than tracking transfers to parents or other kin if the husband is the primary provider to the household. In other social roles (as adult child or sibling), the migrant's economic contributions may not be specified in reports of household income if they are not substantial.

Despite these valid reasons to study the transfer of remittances within households of procreation, the question of whether children remit to their parents' households remains important. Literature on intergenerational transfers indicates that parents and children exchange economic resources across the life course. Research in the United States suggests that parents continue to give more to their children in adulthood than they receive from them (see Cooney and Uhlenberg 1992), but children's contributions may come at critical times, such as during health emergencies, after the death of one parent, or during a move to another household (Hogan and Eggebeen 1995).

EXPLANATIONS OF TRANSFER BEHAVIOR

Various theories have been posited to explain the motivation to transfer earnings from children to parents. The most common explanations considered include altruism, reciprocity, and strategic investment. Altruism as a motive for transfers is corollary to the idea of the household as a moral economy, introduced by Becker (1991) and described in chapter 2. In the altruistic case, the utility function of parents influences the utilities of their adult children (Becker 1974). Children are motivated to contribute to a pool of shared resources because of their altruistic feelings toward kin, and the preference to contribute is constant across children within a family, even if resources are not distributed evenly (see Pezzin and Schone 2000). That is, all children are equally likely to have the preference to contribute, if not the means. In the case of migration, an example of altruistically-motivated transfers exists in the literature on agricultural households using migration to diversify risk and develop private economic alternatives in the absence of insurance and sound markets. However, empirical tests have found little support for the model of "pure altruism," and have sought alternative explanations of the transfer motive (Lillard and Willis 1997; but see Logan and Spitze 1995; Pezzin and Schone 2000).

The second explanation, reciprocity, takes various forms. In the case of the parental repayment hypothesis, those children in whom parents made greater investments will be more likely to contribute to the parental household, both because they are indebted to the parents and because their human capital is greater. The most frequent empirical test of the repayment hypothesis asks whether children with more education than their siblings transfer more earnings to parents, controlling for earnings (see Lillard and Willis 1997 for an example). Another form of reciprocity is payment to parents in anticipation of eventual bequests of land or property. The examples described in chapter 2 (Lucas and Stark 1985; Stark and Lucas 1988) speak to such a contractual arrangement between parents and children in which the benefits from migration accrue to different parties over time.

A third explanation is the exchange motive for transfers, or strategic investment (Cox 1987). Under this hypothesis, children provide services to their parents in exchange for cash transfers. As long as the parents have more than one child to choose from, they will seek services from children who require the least remuneration. Children requiring the smallest transfers are hypothesized to be those with the lowest opportunity costs or lowest earnings, because children with more income will have more to sacrifice and less to gain from exchanging services for transfers.

This hypothesis is extended to consider remittances as a service children provide to parents, perhaps in exchange for financial assistance to cross the border and become established as a migrant, or for financial support provided to the child's own family while the migrant is away. In this case, children with the fewest opportunities for wage labor in the sending country would be the expected remitters. This extension of the exchange hypothesis is in contrast to the idea that migrant-sending households maximize the probability of remittance receipt by sending the potentially biggest earners abroad. Rather, the migrants who send remittances to parents are not making the most money in absolute terms, but are earning more relative to what they would have made in the sending community. In the case of Mexico-U.S. migration, migrant daughters may be the more likely children to remit to parents if, vis-à-vis sons, they receive greater relative earnings in the United States compared to what they would have earned in Mexico. To the extent that daughters in Mexico are more likely than sons to engage in temporary or occasional low-wage labor in the informal sector or in piecework produced at home, their potential earnings in the United States could be far greater than what they would earn in Mexico. A selection process for U.S.-bound daughters also may be operating, such that daughters with more skills or education who stand to earn higher income within Mexico are selected to migrate internally to the best-paying jobs, and those daughters who would have relatively low earnings within Mexico are selected to work in the United States, where they will earn more in lower-skill occupations.

Reciprocity and exchange theories imply variation among children from the same family in terms of their preference and ability to transfer income to parents. In the case of reciprocity, children with higher education or with more to gain from a specific bequest are more likely to provide cash transfers than their siblings. In the case of exchange, children with more of their own financial resources will have the least incentive to offer any services to parents, and parents will seek out the child with the fewest resources to provide services. In either case, variation in transfer patterns is likely to be divided along a few axes, including the sex, marital status, and age of adult children. Observed differences in cash transfers between sons and daughters and between married and unmarried children may be explained in part by the absence or presence of such motives among those children.

In addition to considering the *motive* to transfer earnings from children to parents, we must also consider children's *ability* to remit. For migrants, this will be a function of earnings, cost of living, and competing demands, as well as bargaining strength in the household in the destination country in order to dispense with one's earnings as one chooses (Lee, Parish, and Willis 1994). As with motives there will be variation in the ability of adult child migrants to remit. The data used in the forthcoming analyses addresses two of these aspects of ability to transfer migrants' earnings to parents.

First, the occupations that parents report their children hold indicate children's potential to earn sufficient wages to remit. Second, marital status represents whether children are subject to demands from another family or from children. Although migrants will maintain their social roles as adult children to their parents for life, marriage is expected to mark the tipping point between responsibilities to households of origin and procreation. From the child's perspective, this means that she will allocate her resources differently as she ages. From the parents' perspective, this means that they will enter middle age with unfettered access to the resources their children can provide, but as they age and as children marry, their access to those resources will diminish. In the context of migration, this means that parents will benefit the most from their children's migration early, when children have little experience and, perhaps, low earnings.

DATA

The analyses in this chapter test the competing hypotheses of motives to transfer earnings described above, controlling for ability, and consider the role of migrant children in explaining patterns of cash transfer receipt. Analyses are based on data from the eight communities included in the 1996 wave of the HMS. The dependent variable is the dollar value of cash transfers received from children in the preceding month. Matched data on household characteristics and migration prevalence from the MMP were collected in 1994 and 1995. Using the

1994/95 data to predict transfer receipt in 1996 introduces the risk of missing transfer events where migrant children who have returned in the period between surveys were transferring money while in the United States. Conversely, children who migrated after the MMP interview and are still in the United States at interview will not be counted among the migrants who are potential remitters to the parental household. However, using the data in this arrangement does establish a direction of causality, from migration to transfer receipt.

The sample is restricted to parental households where the head has at least one child age 15 or over at the time of the MMP interview. As in analyses in preceding chapters, the sample is further restricted to include households with married or cohabiting heads in their first union. This restriction produces a sample that is slightly younger with more migrant children than would be the case if female-headed households were included. The final sample includes 529 households.

Tests of Hypotheses

The quantitative analysis uses indicators of the transfer motives described above to explain variation in the probability and size of transfer receipt among parental households with or without adult children in the United States.[36] Table 6.1 describes the expected associations between the independent and dependent variables implied by each hypothesis. (Grey cells indicate no hypothesized association.) If the altruism hypothesis holds, individual ability would be the primary factor explaining whether children transfer earnings to parents. To assess children's ability to make transfers, two indicators of children's employment in skilled occupations reflect children's earning capacity. The first indicator is the proportion of all adult children in skilled occupations. The second is the number of children currently

---

[36]Ideally, an analysis would assess an individual child's probability of remitting, instead of assessing the probability that a household would receive cash transfers from children when some children are in the United States. The data available in the HMS for such an analysis are incomplete: they include reports on contributions from up to two migrant children, although many families have more children abroad; and the information available to identify the child who contributes does not appear to correspond to the household roster.

Table 6.1 Expected effects of measures of parental household predicting any cash transfer from child to parent (Shaded cells indicate no expected effect specified)

Characteristics of household head and spouse	Altruism	Reciprocity	Exchange
Age of household head	+		+
Spouse in normal, good, or very good health	-		-
Household head employed	-		-
Spouse employed	-		-
Characteristics of the household			
Household SES	-	+	-
Land ownership		+	-
Household size			
Number of minors	+		
Number of coresident adults	+		
Average education of adult children (years)	No effect	+	-
Percentage of children in skilled occupations	+	+	-
Migration prevalence/experience in the household			
Household head has US experience		+	
Migrant children are skilled	+	+	-
Migrant children have more education than sibs	No effect	+	-
Migrant children are male	No effect		-
Migrant children are married	No effect		-

employed in skilled occupations in the United States. The inclusion of both variables permits an evaluation of the independent effect of skilled children's migration, controlling for the level of skilled employment among children from the household overall. Skilled occupations include managerial positions, office workers, technicians, skilled manual labor, and managerial positions. The comparison category includes adult children not in the labor force, and children working in such occupations as street vending, unskilled manual labor, service sector positions, and agriculture.

If the reciprocity hypothesis prevails, households will receive cash transfers where parents have given some children preferential access to resources, including education and property. Children who have received more education relative to their siblings may engage in the repayment model of reciprocity. To account for whether children with more education relative to their siblings are more likely to provide transfers to their parents, two indicators of education are included. The first is the average number of years of schooling among children in the household. The second is the number of children with more than average education in the United States.

Where households have a relatively high level of assets that may not be divided equally, those children more likely to eventually receive the assets may engage in anticipatory reciprocity by providing cash transfers with the expectation of eventually receiving a bequest. The household's socioeconomic status (measured as an index of assets) and land ownership status (owning at least 5 hectares) are included as indicators of heritable property.[1] These indicators of wealth are

---

[1] The socioeconomic status (SES) index used here (derived from Donato and Kanaiaupuni 2000) includes four components and separates out land ownership. The four components are whether the household head owns the home where his family resides; whether the household owns a business; whether the home has at least 5 rooms (including the kitchen and bathrooms); and whether the home has a tile floor (vs. a cement or dirt floor). The SES index used in chapters 4 and 5 excluded the number of rooms and type of floor, and included an indicator of whether the household possessed a landholding of at least 5 hectares. That information was not available retrospectively and so could not be used in the analysis in chapter 4. Although the cross-sectional analysis in chapter 5 might have included those additional indicators, they were

interacted with measures of migration prevalence in the household to determine whether households with migrant children are more likely to receive transfers when some children stand to inherit something of value.

Finally, the number of married and unmarried sons and daughters in the United States are taken into account in four different variables (married sons, married daughters, unmarried sons, unmarried daughters). Households with unmarried children in the United States are expected to receive cash transfers more often than those with married children abroad because unmarried children will have fewer competing responsibilities. Children's gender is taken into account to test the exchange hypothesis, which predicts that children who migrate are not necessarily the household's biggest earners, but rather are those who have the most to gain relative to what they would have received had they remained in Mexico to work. Working daughters more than sons are expected to earn more in the United States relative to what they would have earned in Mexico, to the extent that female workers in Mexico are overrepresented in lower-paying occupations in the informal sector and in homework. Households with unmarried daughters in the United States are expected to receive larger cash transfers than those with married daughters both because married daughters' earnings may be diverted elsewhere and because married daughters are less likely to work at all.

Other Predictors

Several characteristics of the parents and their household are thought to influence cash transfers from children. These factors include economic need, health status, and household composition (Hogan, Eggebeen, and Clogg 1993).

To measure economic need, indicators from the MMP that have been used in preceding analyses are used: the age of the household head; the employment status of the head; and the spouse's labor force

---

excluded so that the analysis in chapters 4 and 5 could be compared directly. The richer indicator of SES is used here to determine whether children respond to differences in the quality of home ownership and to the availability of land, which has both productive and commercial value.

status. These indicators are included in addition to the SES index and the measure of land ownership described above.

To measure the presence of health problems in the household, a dichotomous measure of female health status from the HMS is included. This covariate is based on a 5-scale item asking the respondent to report what she perceives her overall status to be. The response categories include very good (1); good (2); average (3); bad (4); and very bad (5).[2] The universal self-report measure of health has been found to be a valid and reliable measure of respondent health when compared to health assessments by medical practitioners (Idler and Benyamini 1997). The majority of women (86 percent) report being in average or good health. In this research, The five-category variables is collapsed into a dichotomous variable indicating a positive health assessment, coded very good/good/average=1, bad/very bad=0.

To measure household composition, counts of minor children and coresident adults (including the head, spouse/partner, adult children, and other household members) are included. The number of minor children is included as a measure of dependency, although it can also be interpreted as a measure of the parental household's life-cycle. The two interpretations have significant conceptual overlap. The count of coresident adult children indicates the resources available to parents within the household for time and money (but for a study of adult coresident children in economic need, see White 1994). Although this variable is included only as a control measure here, it deserves further study in a selection model that would estimate jointly the probability of transfer receipt and coresidence with children, as there may be an endogenous relationship.

Descriptive analysis

Table 6.2 shows that there are differences in the composition and character of households receiving child-to-parent transfers compared to those that are not receiving transfers.

Households that receive child-to-parent transfers appear to be in a similar life cycle stage to households not receiving transfers,

---

[2] The response wording in the Spanish language instrument is "Muy buena, buena, normal, mal, o muy mal."

Table 6.2 Characteristics of parental households, by receipt of cash transfers from children, unweighted means and frequencies, HMS and MMP93

	All		No contributions		Any contributions	
	Mean	SD	Mean	SD	Mean	SD
Household receives any contribution from children	0.563	0.496				
Value of transfer from children, in US$	78.559	144.756	0	0	139.46	169.503
Age of household head	55.609	11.591	52.623	12.144	57.923 *	10.599
Household head is employed	0.898	0.303	0.918		0.883	
Spouse is employed	0.229	0.420	0.277		0.191 *	
No. of minors in household	1.403	1.615	1.446	1.63	1.369	1.605
No. of adults in household	3.864	1.742	3.753	1.705	3.95	1.768
Spouse is in good health	0.860	0.347	0.883		0.842	
SES index (0-4)	2.327	0.777	2.381	0.809	2.285	0.749
Household owns 5 ha of land	0.270	0.445	0.173		0.346 *	
Average years of adult children's education	7.962	2.856	8.593	3.143	7.473 *	2.509
Prop. Of children in skilled occupations	0.183	0.256	0.16	0.258	0.201	0.254
Proportion of households with family members in United States						
Household head	0.062		0.082		0.047	
Any children w/> avg. education	0.251		0.138		0.339 *	
Any children in skilled occupations	0.126		0.065		0.175 *	

133

Table 6.2 Characteristics of parental households, by receipt of cash transfers from children, unweighted means and frequencies, HMS and MMP93, continued

	All		No contributions		Any contributions	
	Mean	SD	Mean	SD	Mean	SD
Any unmarried sons	0.199		0.103		0.272 *	
Any unmarried daughters	0.069		0.013		0.114 *	
Any married sons	0.196		0.113		0.261 *	
Any married daughters	0.151		0.091		0.198 *	
MMP community number						
36	0.157		0.209		0.117 *	
37	0.117		0.087		0.141	
38	0.155		0.178		0.138	
39	0.096		0.074		0.114	
44	0.091		0.04		0.131 *	
45	0.164		0.113		0.205 *	
47	0.157		0.234		0.097 *	
48	0.062		0.069		0.057	
N	529		231		298	

*Group differences are statistically significant at p<.05

although heads in receiving households are about 2.3 years older on average (57.923 years) and slightly less often in the labor force.[1] Few women work overall (22.9 percent), but women work less frequently in the households receiving transfers. The spouse/partner of the household is in good health slightly less often in recipient households (84.2 percent vs. 88.3 percent), but the difference is not statistically significant.

Households receiving transfers had slightly lower socioeconomic status in 1994 and 1995 compared to those that were not receiving transfers in 1996 (2.28 vs. 2.38 on a scale of 0 to 4). However, they much more often own land. Almost 35 percent of receiving households have at least five hectares of land, compared to only 17.3 percent of non-receiving households. Rural households frequently use remittances to bolster agricultural production (Durand, Parrado, and Massey 1996), and this finding might indicate that children contribute earnings more often to achieve such ends.

Households receiving transfers have slightly more minor and adult members than do households not receiving transfers, although the differences are not statistically significant at the .05 level. These figures point to a greater *supply* of income sources as well as greater sources of *demand* in the households receiving transfers. Larger families obviously provide more sources for income contributions, although typically, the chance that any one family member will contribute is less than in smaller families (Pezzin and Schone 2000).

The household groups experience comparable levels of dependency. The ratio between minor household members and adult family members is the household dependency ratio, which will be smaller where there are fewer minor members and/or more adult members. In the current case, households not receiving transfers have a dependency ratio of .385 (1.446 minors/3.753 adults). The dependency ratio in households receiving transfers is .346 (1.369/3.95), or about 10 percent smaller.

---

[1] The similarity in life cycle stage between the two groups may reflect the restrictions imposed in selecting the analytic sample. When households where the head has been married more than once are included, the head in receiving households is five years older on average and significantly less often employed compared to heads in non-recipient households.

The proportion of households with some children in the United States is two times greater where parents receive transfers compared to households where they do not; nearly half of recipient households (140 of 298 households) have at least one child abroad, compared to twenty percent of non-receiving households (45 of 231 households). The comparison between the proportions of unmarried children in the two groups is especially striking: 27.2 percent of recipient households have sons in the United States, and over 11 percent have daughters there, compared to 10.3 percent and 1.3 percent respectively in the non-recipient group.

Looking at married and unmarried sons and daughters separately reveals variation in their contributions to parental households (see table 6.3). Seventy-five percent of households with a migrant child in the United States receive some income from children, but not all children send money with the same frequency or in the same amount. In order to distinguish how contributions are associated with the sex and marital status of children, four groups are contrasted: households with only unmarried sons in the United States; only married sons in the United States; only unmarried daughters in the United States; and only married daughters there. Households in the first category are the least frequent recipients of transfers (69.6 percent), while those with only unmarried daughters in the United States receive remittances most often (92.3 percent).[2] However, there are relatively few households with only unmarried daughters in the United States compared to other arrangements, suggesting that this arrangement is not a common source of cash transfers. When parents with migrant unmarried sons do receive money, it is in greater amounts than what parents with unmarried daughters receive. The average contribution from children in households with only unmarried migrant sons in the United States, given that they receive anything, is $213.44. Households with only unmarried daughters in the United States receive $181.33 on average, a

---

[2] More precisely, when sons of one marital status *travel without siblings in any other sex/marital status category* their parents receive money less often than the parents of unmarried daughters who travel without siblings in other such categories.

Table 6.3 Household income receipt from children, HMS and MMP93

Proportion of households receiving income from children, 1996

All households	Households w/ any child migrant	Households w/ male migrants only	Households w/ female migrants only
0.563	0.751	0.729	0.786
		Only single: 0.696	Only single: 0.923
		Only married: 0.707	Only married: 0.714

Average conditional household income receipt from children, in U.S. dollars (pesos/7.5), 1996

All households	Households w/ any child migrant	Households w/ male migrants only	Households w/ female migrants only
78.559	174.03	154.06	168.06
		Only single: 213.44	Only single: 181.33
		Only married: 106.38	Only married: 158.50

difference of about 15 percent. Households with only married children in the United States receive contributions from children at about the same rate as those households with unmarried migrant sons (70.7 percent with married sons abroad and 71.4 percent with married daughters abroad), but the average payments are much smaller ($106.38 for married sons and $158.50 for married daughters).

Multivariate Analysis

The multivariate analysis uses a Tobit model to estimate the probability of receiving any cash transfer from children, and if so, the value of the transfer. The independent variables included in the model describe the attributes of the household and its members and test competing theories about children's motivation to transfer income to parents.

Tobit analysis is useful when the dependent variable has a number of its values clustered at a limiting value, in this case 0 (Long 1997). The Tobit method uses all of the observations in a sample, both those at the limit (those not receiving any cash transfers), and those above it (those receiving a transfer), and is considered a better alternative to using only those observations with values on the dependent variable above the limit. It models the probability that a household that did not receive a transfer might have received one under a different set of conditions such that the threshold for receiving transfers were lower. While some households will never receive a transfer, others might receive them periodically, but not during the month of interview, and others may receive an occasional, unscheduled transfer. Each type of household has a different real probability of receiving a transfer, although they were all observed to receive nothing in the month of interview. The Tobit method exploits this variation between households to produce less biased estimators than ordinary least squares (OLS) methods would produce.

The Tobit model assumes an underlying latent (i.e., unobserved) dependent variable y_i^* which represents the propensity of households to receive cash transfers. The latent variable is related to right-hand-side variables in the standard linear regression fashion:

$$y_i^* = \sum B_j x_{ij} + u_i, i = 1, 2, \ldots, n$$

where n is the number of observations, the x_{ij} are independent variables, the β_j are parameters to be estimated, and u_i is a normally-distributed error term with mean 0 and variance σ^2. However, we observe not y_i^* but y_i, such that:

$$y_i \begin{cases} = 0 \\ = \sum B_j x_{ij} + u_i \\ = 25 \end{cases} \quad \text{if} \quad \begin{cases} y_i^* \leq 0 \\ 0 < y_i^* < 25 \\ y_i^* \geq 25 \end{cases}$$

The parameters j and their standard errors can be estimated by maximum likelihood methods. The parameters may be interpreted as the effect of a one-unit change in the independent variable x_{ij} on the latent variable, y_i^*. The standard deviation of the error term σ indicates whether there is substantial clustering at the limits. Where σ is high (i.e., greater than the width of the observed interval), many of the observations in the sample are clustered at limiting values.

Although the Tobit regression model corrects for censoring by positing the normally distributed latent variable, y_i^*, we only observe the variable y_i, which is bounded at the lower value of 0. To get a practical interpretation of the results based on the regression models, two quantities are reported in addition to the coefficients and standard errors. The first is the change in the probability of receiving a transfer at all, given a one-unit change in the value of x_{ij} when all other x_j's are held at their means. The second is an estimate of the change in the expected value of y_i that accounts for censoring given a one-unit change in x_{ij}. The estimation accounts for censoring by weighting the value of the coefficient associated with x_j by the probability that y_i is uncensored. This is reported in table 6.4 as the change in E(Y), or the change in the expected value of y_i.

The altruism hypothesis predicts that all children have an equal preference to make transfers, but not equal means. Children in skilled occupations and children not exposed to competing demands may be more likely to make transfers to parents than children in unskilled occupations or children not in the labor force. First, the proportion of children in the household employed in skilled occupations would be associated with the likelihood that a household will receive a transfer from children if the altruism hypothesis were to hold. Controlling for children's overall skill level, the number of children employed in skilled occupations in the United States represents the extent to which remittances may provide a source of transfers in an altruistic model. Second, households with unmarried children may be more likely than those with married children to receive transfers if married children divert earnings to satisfy the demands of their own families of procreation or those of the families into which they have married.

The analytical results provide partial support for the altruism hypothesis: the availability of skilled children is not associated with transfers in the current analysis, but the prevalence of unmarried children in the United States is. In regard to the first test of the hypothesis, the coefficient associated with the proportion of children in skilled occupations is not significant, and the coefficient associated with the number of skilled children in the United States is negative and significant at the .10 level, indicating that the number of skilled migrant children is weakly associated with diminished transfers. But the number of unmarried sons and unmarried daughters in the United States is positively associated with the size of transfers the parental household receives. The value of the coefficient associated with the number of unmarried sons in the United States is 93.510. For each additional unmarried son in the United States, the probability of receiving transfers in the parental household increases by .20 (when all other covariates are held at their means). Given that a household receives any transfers, the expected value of the dependent variable (E(Y)) shows that the addition of an unmarried son abroad increases the value of the transfer by $34.17. The magnitude of the effect for unmarried daughters is even greater (see below), but the number of married sons or daughters is unrelated to cash transfers.

The reciprocity hypothesis predicts that children will be more likely to make transfers to parents when they, relative to their siblings, have received more investments from parents or when they anticipate benefiting from investments or transfers in the future. Education is treated as a prior investment. Controlling for the average years of education among all children in the parental household, a count of the number of children with more than average education in the United States provides a test of the reciprocity hypothesis. The hypothesis is not supported by the analysis. The magnitude of the coefficient associated with the number of children with greater-than-average education is negative, relatively small, and not statistically significant.

Table 6.4 Results from a Tobit regression estimating the value of cash transfers from children to parents, HMS and MMP93

	B	SE	Change in Pr(y>0)	Change in E(Y)
Age of household head	1.440	1.080	0.003	0.526
Household head is employed	-85.079	32.158 *	-0.177	-34.705
Spouse is employed	-19.663	23.769	-0.042	-7.064
No. of minors in household	10.381	6.693	0.022	3.793
No. of adults in household	12.321	5.613 *	0.026	4.502
Spouse is in good health	-29.257	26.299	-0.062	-11.061
SES index (0-4)	17.596	12.578	0.038	6.430
Household owns 5 ha of land	70.512	24.757 *	0.149	27.182
Average years of adult children's education	-6.251	4.210	-0.013	-2.284
Prop. Of children in skilled occupations	59.289	45.327	0.127	21.665
Proportion of households with family members in United States				
Household head	4.861	42.819	0.010	1.788
Any children w/> avg. education	-13.894	12.538	-0.030	-5.077
Any children in skilled occupations	-29.893	16.305	-0.064	-10.923
Any unmarried sons	93.510	16.110 *	0.200	34.170
Any unmarried daughters	143.421	31.971 *	0.306	52.408

Table 6.4 Results from a Tobit regression estimating the value of cash transfers from

children to parents, HMS and MMP93, continued

	B	SE		Change in Pr(y>0)	Change in E(Y)
Any married sons	16.991	14.059		0.036	6.209
Any married daughters	27.326	15.486		0.058	9.985
MMP community number					
36	-184.913	39.626	*	-0.361	-55.852
37	-105.804	40.954	*	-0.218	-34.083
38	-134.330	39.081	*	-0.273	-42.584
39	-92.597	41.428	*	-0.192	-30.099
45	-91.281	36.743	*	-0.191	-30.322
47	-176.470	39.195	*	-0.347	-53.732
48	-139.417	49.308	*	-0.277	-42.176
Intercept	32.588	103.896			
Sigma	186.904	8.075			
N	529				

*p<.05

The anticipatory version of the reciprocity hypothesis was tested in models not shown here. In 8 separate models, the household's land ownership status and socioeconomic index were interacted with the number of unmarried and married sons and daughters in the United States. None of the interaction terms was significant, meaning that households with migrant children are no more likely to receive cash transfers from children when the household possesses land or other assets that may be inherited by children in the future.

The exchange hypothesis predicts that parents will be most likely to receive cash transfers from children when they have invested in children who would otherwise have relatively low earnings. In the context of children's migration, it is hypothesized that children who would receive a relatively higher return to earnings in the United States than in Mexico may get help from parents to defray the costs of migration in exchange for the eventual transfer of earnings. This hypothesis is tested by including four covariates as separate counts of the number of married and unmarried sons and daughters in the United States. Based on the analysis in chapter 4, daughters are expected to require more assistance from within the family compared to sons because they are less involved in the social networks built around migration outside of the household. Married children, and especially married daughters, are expected to require fewer investments in migration from parents if they are able to draw on resources from in-laws or from their own asset accumulation. The exchange hypothesis is supported by the analysis: households with unmarried daughters in the United States are much more likely to receive transfers from children. Households with unmarried sons in the United States are also very likely to receive cash transfers, but the magnitude of the effect of daughters' migration is much greater, translating to larger transfers ($E(Y)=52.41$) and a large increase in the probability of receipt with the addition of an unmarried daughter in the United States (change in Pr $y>0=.31$).

Attributes of the household that are associated with the receipt of cash transfers from children include the labor force status of the household head, the number of adults in the household, and land ownership. The head's employment is negatively associated with cash transfers, while household size and land ownership are positively associated. Each association is consistent with previous research on intergenerational transfers from children to parents. Where the head is unemployed, household earnings are likely to diminish; children's contributions compensate for the head's lost earnings. Where there are more adults in the household, including more adult children, there are likely to be more contributors to the household economy. Finally, the positive relationship between land ownership and the receipt of transfers from children is consistent with the finding that households that hold land tend to invest remittances in that land. Children may be more likely to transfer money to parents when that money is put to economically productive use.

DISCUSSION

Descriptive and multivariate analyses show that parents are much more likely to receive cash transfers when at least one unmarried son or daughter was in the United States one to two years prior to interview, and that the size of those transfers is greater than what other households receive. Households with married sons or daughters in the United States are no more likely than other households to receive transfers from children. The absence of effects for married children contrasts research on migrant remittances that found married children are frequent remitters, but does not consider to whose household those children are remitting (Durand, Parrado, and Massey 1996). These findings together suggest that married children remit their earnings outside the parental home.

Comparing the contributions from sons and daughters, the multivariate analysis reveals slightly more complicated transfer patterns than the descriptive results showed. The main conclusion from the discussion of descriptive results was that households with daughters in the United States tend to receive transfers more often than those with sons there, but the transfer amounts are smaller on average. Although no household has more than two unmarried migrant daughters, the probability of transfer receipt increases by .62 and the expected value of transfers increases by over $100 ((E(Y)$52.40)*2=104.80). In comparison, a similar probability and expected value of transfers would occur only when there were three or more unmarried sons in the United States. These results strengthen the conclusion from the descriptive results, with the added information that parents receive transfers more often and in greater amounts with fewer unmarried daughters than sons in the United States.

Differences in occupations and living arrangements between unmarried sons and daughters might explain the tendency for households with U.S. daughters to receive money relatively often. In the current data, the majority of unmarried sons are employed in unspecified unskilled labor, while daughters work as *domésticas*, or housekeepers/nannies in private homes. *Doméstica* encompasses a range of occupational categories, including live-in and live-out housekeepers, as well as housekeepers who clean homes for a list of clients on a routine basis. While live-in housekeepers might be expected to have the fewest financial demands in the United States, and therefore the greatest opportunity to remit, there is evidence against this explanation (Hondagneu-Sotelo 2001). In an ethnographic study of the three types of *domésticas,* Hondagneu-Sotelo concludes that women working in live-in situations receive extremely low pay, and that they are frequently women who have recently arrived in the United States with no options or resources to find other work and living arrangements. This group, then, might be among the *least* likely to remit. Those daughters who transfer earnings may be in live-out or client-based housekeeping employment or in other occupations.

Overall, these analyses have produced two results. First, parents with daughters in the United States receive significant cash transfers from children, equal to or greater than those received when sons are abroad. Second, both the altruism and exchange hypotheses were supported by the analysis. Households with unmarried children are more likely to receive transfers than those with married children, suggesting that those with the fewest competing commitments make transfers to parents. This finding provides some support for the altruism hypothesis. But the significantly larger likelihood and size of contributions from daughters compared to sons suggest that daughters are contributing a larger share of their earnings, assuming that sons and daughters' earnings are comparable. This disparity indicates that sons and daughters have different motivations to remit, with daughters perhaps reimbursing parents for the expenses incurred by migration. One conclusion to draw from this finding is that remittance streams might be divided by gender in the United States, with daughters responding to motivation to remit to parents and sons remitting to their own families or saving. Because women's labor migration is a recent but growing phenomenon, this finding may represent only a cohort effect, in which women who are new to migration streams are maintaining closer ties to family initially. Further analysis is required to establish whether this is a long-term gender-based division. An alternative explanation could be that daughters migrate for earnings only as a last resort, when parents need the money. However, interactions between such indicators of need and women's migration were not significant.

This research has contributed to our understanding of the role of migration in intergenerational transfers, a relationship that has been the subject of relatively little scholarship. In addition, the results from this project suggest that migrant children maintain different roles and expectations in their relationships with parents in adulthood. However, the study does have some limitations.

First, we cannot establish a direct relationship between children's migration and transfer receipt by parents. That is, the data do not indicate which child sent money to her parents, so we cannot rule out the possibility that the observed relationship between migration and transfers may be only associational, and explained by another, unobserved process. Second, the data lack information on the context in which children decide whether to remit, including other economic pressures, earnings, and control over money. In general terms, the analysis suffers from our ability to see migrant children only as their parents' children, and not as adults making choices and trade-offs between family and other responsibilities. Despite these limitations, this study has identified some patterns in the frequency and magnitude of cash transfers form children to parents with or without children in the United States. This potentially opens a new area of research bridging the literature on intergenerational transfers and migration.

CHAPTER 7

Conclusion
Migrants as Adult Children and Siblings

The objective of the preceding chapters was to describe how parents, adult children, and siblings in Mexico relate to each other in the context of international migration. Much of the research on international migration considers migrants as spouses and parents for whom migration shapes households of procreation. The current research has shown that the parental household is integral to the inception of the migration process, and that in their social roles as adult children, migrants reshape and sustain the parental household. This final chapter reviews the research questions posed at the outset, the conclusions suggested by quantitative analysis, and the implications for future work at the intersection of research on international migration and intergenerational relations.

The first research question asked which children from a common parental household becomes migrants. The purpose of the analysis was to focus on the way common background characteristics interact with the attributes of individual household members to produce distinct chances of migration. The motivations for migration that were considered included economic need, the availability of kin, and social capital. Each of these motivations was hypothesized to operate differently for children from the same household depending on their sex and birth order. To take those differences into account analytically, sons and daughters from urban and rural households were considered in separate analysis pools.

The results show that migration by sons is associated with economic need in the household to the extent that the number of dependent children in the household positively influences the odds that an adult son will become a migrant. Neither daughters' labor nor non-labor migration is associated with the indicators of economic need in the parental household. These results suggest that daughters' migration is not a last-resort strategy employed by economically strained households; rather, daughters may be more likely to become migrants when the household has an adequate financial cushion to finance daughters' migration and to absorb the loss of their income and labor contributions.

The availability of kin, and particularly the availability of adult sisters, also positively predicts sons' migration, but the number of brothers and sisters' is unrelated to daughters' migration. Gender differences in the results suggest that the availability of kin does not represent potential for the direct substitution of labor in the household. Rather, for sons, daughters' availability may represent a labor supply reserve from which the family draws when other children are absent.

In terms of social capital, almost all children are positively influenced to migrate by their siblings' migration experience and by the accumulated migration experience in the community. However, important variations emerged. First, sons are more influenced by their brothers' migration experience, and daughters are more influenced by that of their sisters. This distinction suggests that access to migration-related social capital and the ability to put that capital to use falls along gender lines, even within the relatively intimate setting of the parental household. Second, not all children within a household are equally influenced by siblings' migration experience. Younger sons and daughters are slightly less likely to migrate when their older brothers and sisters have already begun migrating. Finally, children in urban areas are more influenced by their siblings' migration and less influenced by the level of migration prevalence in their community compared to children in rural areas, perhaps because the social networks associated with migration prevalence are less established in urban areas.

The second question asked whether children's migration influences the organization of the parental household. Migration competes with marriage and labor force entry as a cause for homeleaving by children.

In households where children migrate, nonmigrant children might choose to delay or accelerate their own homeleaving in order to sustain the parental household. In the current research, the household was conceptualized as the point where the interests of parents and children potentially compete. Parents might have an economic incentive to retain adult children in the household in order to receive earnings and labor contributions from them, thus extending the productive quality of the consolidated household (Gonzalez de la Rocha 1994). Adult children, on the other hand, might wish to establish independent households in which to raise a nuclear family.

The analysis shows that in urban households, daughters' migration is positively associated with their nonmigrant brothers' and sisters' homeleaving. However, there is a caveat for married daughters; although marriage powerfully predicts homeleaving, married daughters are slightly less likely to live outside the parental household when a sister is abroad. In rural households, daughters' migration is *negatively* associated with their nonmigrant sisters' homeleaving and is unrelated to nonmigrant brothers' homeleaving. Also in contrast to the finding for children from urban households, married nonmigrant daughters are slightly *more* likely to live outside the parental household when a sister is abroad. (See table 5.4 for a comparison of the probability of homeleaving for children with various attributes with or without migrant sisters.)

The third question considers migrants as participants with parents, siblings, and kin in an ongoing exchange of resources. Specifically, the research considered whether parents with children in the United States receive earnings transfers from children, and if so, from which children. The analysis considered various motives for children to transfer earnings to parents, and asked whether international migration makes a difference in the probability of receiving a transfer and the size of the transfer.

Three motives for children to transfer earnings to parents were considered: altruism, reciprocity, and exchange. Households are more likely to receive transfers from children when they have unmarried sons or unmarried daughters in the United States. The finding that unmarried children's migration has a stronger association with transfers than does married children's migration suggests support for the altruism hypothesis, because unmarried children have fewer competing responsibilities and therefore may have a greater ability to remit. The probability of receiving earnings with unmarried daughters abroad is higher compared to that for unmarried sons. This pattern suggests support for the exchange hypothesis, assuming that daughters earn proportionally more in the United States than they would in Mexico vis-à-vis sons.

Overall, the analytical chapters have described the parental household as a setting where individuals engage in the significant exchange of material and social resources in their roles as parents, children, and siblings. Children respond to siblings' migration experience in the decision to become migrants themselves, and children's migration is associated with both the composition of and the earnings sources available to the parental household. Much research on the effects of international migration on families in Mexico has implicitly focused on families of procreation by considering how marriage, fertility, and asset building are transformed. Parental households also should be considered as dynamic units where migration transforms economic and social organization.

In the context of the parental household, gender differences in the experience of migration reflect differences between sons and daughters. Consistently, the analytical results showed that daughters are more engaged with the parental household in regard to migration than were sons: daughters are more influenced than sons by their siblings' migration experience; daughters' migration is associated with their siblings' homeleaving, but sons' migration is not; and unmarried daughters' migration is most strongly associated with the likelihood that parental households receive income transfers from children. Furthermore, the availability of adult sisters strongly predicts sons' migration, suggesting that daughters represent a flexible labor supply in the parental household. A large body of research has shown how women's migration experience is distinctive from men's in terms of social networks, timing, context, and employment. The preceding research adds to that literature by highlighting another way in which women's migration is distinctive in terms of its inception, economic role, and consequences for the composition of the parental household.

In chapter 2, three models of household functioning were posited: the moral economy model, the household strategies model, and the household bargaining model. The moral economy is characterized by household members' efforts to jointly maximize utility. The household strategies model incorporates household members' dynamic roles in response to changing external conditions and household priorities. The household bargaining model asserts that rather than behaving as a rational, altruistic unit, individual actors in households have competing self-interests, and conflicts that arise are resolved based on the distribution of power in the household. The preceding research provides some insight into the question of which model best describes the migrant-sending parental household, although conclusions are based almost entirely on inference. A more thorough investigation would require longitudinal data that includes information reported by various actors in the household about how the migration decision is made and about who is perceived to benefit from migration.

In terms of household composition, urban households appear to fragment in the context of migration, while rural households are somewhat more likely to retain members when daughters are abroad. This finding offers some support for the argument that urban households are characterized by the household bargaining model, while rural households may be described by the moral economy or household strategies model. However, this interpretation relies on the assumption that the consolidated household truly is the most economically viable form of organization in both rural and urban areas.

Unmarried children's migration is associated with income transfers to parents. This pattern is consistent with the moral economy framework to the extent that it represents altruistic behavior on the part of migrant children best able to make transfers. However, the additional finding that daughters' migration is more strongly associated with transfers than is sons' migration suggests that parents use their relative economic power to facilitate daughters' migration and to receive benefits in the form of remittances. While this arrangement does not necessarily imply conflict, it does suggest support for the household bargaining model. This interpretation is also supported by the observation that daughters more than sons are influenced by the accumulation of social capital within the household to initiate migration, indicating that daughters' migration may be enabled by inputs from the family, with the understanding that the family receives the economic benefits of migration in return.

In sum, the preceding research has sought to consider migrants at a life course stage when they identify as adult children and act in the context of the parental household. In order to draw on that perspective, migrants have been considered as sons and daughters as well as workers and spouses. Further studies can enhance research on migration and intergenerational relations by looking in more detail at the specific relationships between parents and children in various economic contexts, historical moments, and social conditions.

REFERENCES

Adelman, Irma and Edward J. Taylor. 1990. "Is structural adjustment with a human face possible?" *Journal of Development Studies* 26:387-407.

Aiken, Leona S. and Stephen G. West. 1991. *Multiple Regression: Testing and Interpreting Interactions*. Thousand Oaks, CA: Sage Publications.

Arizpe, Lourdes. 1982. "Relay Migration and the Survival of the Peasant Household." in *Towards a Political Economy of Urbanization in Third World Countries*, edited by H. I. Safa. Delhi: Oxford University Press.

Becker, Gary S. 1974. "A Theory of Social Interactions." *Journal of Political Economy* 82:1063-1093.

—. 1991. *A Treatise on the Family*. Cambridge, MA: Harvard University Press.

Blank, Susan. 1998. "Hearth and Home: The Living Arrangements of Mexican Immigrants and U.S.-Born Mexican Americans." *Sociological Forum* 13:35-59.

Borjas, George J. 1999. *Heaven's Door: Immigration Policy and the American Economy*. Princeton, NJ: Princeton University Press.

Bouillon, Cesar Patricio, Arianna Loegovini, and Nora Lustig. 2003. "Rising Inequality in Mexico: Household Characteristics and Regional Effects." *The Journal of Development Studies* 39:112-133.

Bourdieu, Pierre and Loic Wacquant. 1992. *An Invitation to Reflexive Sociology*. Chicago: University of Chicago Press.

Boyd, Monica. 1989. "Immigration and Income Security Policies in Canada: Implications for Elderly Immigrant Women." *Population Research and Policy Review* 8:5-24.

Burawoy, Michael. 1976. "The Functions and Reproduction of Migrant Labor: Comparative Material from Southern Africa and the United States." *American Journal of Sociology* 81:1050-1087.

Burr, J.A. and J.E. Mutchler. 1993. "Ethnic Living Arrangements: Cultural Convergence of Cultural Manifestation?" *Social Forces* 71:170-179.

Casique, Irene. 2001. *Power, Autonomy and Division of Labor in Mexican Dual-Earner Families*. Lanham, MD: University Press of America.

CELADE (Comisión Económica para America Latina y El Caribe). 1998. *Demographic Bulletin #62: Latin America, Population Projections 1970-2050* [in Spanish]. Santiago, Chile: Centro Latinoamericano y Caribeno de Demografía.

Cerrutti, Marcela and Douglas S. Massey. 2001. "On the Auspices of Female Migration from Mexico to the United States." *Demography* 38:187-200.

Chan, Angelique and Julie DaVanzo. 1994. "Ethnic Differences in Parents' Coresidence with Adult Children in Peninsular Malaysia." RAND, Santa Monica, CA.

Clark, Rebecca and Douglas Wolf. 1992. "Proximity of Children and Elderly Migration." in *Elderly Migration and Population Redistribution*, edited by A. Rogers. London: Bellhaven Press.

Collins, Jane L. 1985. "Migration and the Life Cycle of Households in Southern Peru." *Urban Anthropology* 14:279-299.

Cooney, Teresa M. and Peter Uhlenberg. 1992. "Support from Parents over the Life Course: The Adult Child's Perspective." *Social Forces* 71:63-84.

Cox, Donald. 1987. "Motives for Private Transfers." *The Journal of Political Economy* 95.

Curran, Sara. 1996. "Intra-Household Exchange Relations: Explanations for Gender Differentials in Education and Migration Outcomes in Thailand." Seattle, WA: Center for Studies in Demography and Ecology, University of Washington.

Cypher, James M. 2001. "Developing Disarticulation Within the Mexican Economy." *Latin American Perspectives* 28:11-37.

DaVanzo, Julie and Frances K. Goldscheider. 1990. "Coming Home Again: Returns to the Parental Home of Young Adults." *Population Studies* 44:241-255.

De Vos, Susan. 1989. "Leaving the Parental Home: Patterns in Six Latin American Countries." *Journal of Marriage and the Family* 51:615-626.

deJanvry, Alain, Gustavo Gordillo, and Elizabeth Sadoulet. 1997. *Mexico's Second Agrarian Reform: Household and Community Responses*. San Diego: Center for U.S.-Mexican Studies at the University of California - San Diego.

DeVos, Susan. 1989. "Leaving the Parental Home: Patterns in Six Latin American Countries." *Journal of Marriage and the Family* 51:615-626.

———. 1995. *Household Composition in Latin America*. New York: Plenum Press.

Dinerman, Ina. 1978. "Patterns of Adaptation Among Households of U.S.-Bound Migrants from Michoacan, Mexico." *International Migration Review* 12:485-501.

Doeringer, Peter B. and Michael J. Piore. 1971. *Internal Labor Markets and Manpower Analysis*. Lexington, MA: DC Health.

Donato, Katharine. 1993. "Current Trends and Patterns of Female Migration: Evidence from Mexico." *International Migration Review* 27:748-771.

Donato, Katharine M., Jorge Durand, and Douglas S. Massey. 1992. "Stemming the Tide? Assessing the Deterrent Effects of IRCA." *Demography* 29:139-157.

Donato, Katharine M. and Shawn M. Kanaiaupuni. 2000. "Women's Status and Demographic Change: The Case of Mexico-U.S. Migration." Pp. 217-242 in *Women, Poverty, and Demographic Change*, edited by B. Garcia. Oxford: Oxford University Press.

Durand, Jorge, Douglas S. Massey, and Rene M. Zenteno. 2001. "Mexican Immigration to the United States: Continuities and Changes." *Latin American Research Review* 36:107-127.

Durand, Jorge, Emilio A. Parrado, and Douglas S. Massey. 1996. "Migradollars and Development: A Reconsideration of the Mexican Case." *International Migration Review* 30:423-444.

El Programa Paisano del Gobierno de Mexico. 2001. "Report on Adolescent and Young Migrants [in Spanish]." vol. 2001. Mexico City: El Programa Paisano del Gobierno de Mexico.

Federal Reserve Bank of Dallas. 2004. "El Paso Business Frontier." El Paso, TX: Federal Reserve Bank of Dallas.

Flores, Eunice Banuelos and Leonor Paz Gomez. 1997. "Changes in Mexican Households (in Spanish)." *Demos* 10:24-26.

Folbre, Nancy. 1986. "Hearts and Spades: Paradigms of Household Economics." *World Development* 14:245-255.

Fussell, Elizabeth and Douglas S. Massey. 2004. "The Limits to Cumulative Causation: International Migration from Mexican Urban Areas." *Demography* 41:151-171.

Gilbertson, Greta A. 1995. "Women's Labor and Enclave Employment: The Case of Dominican and Colombian Women in New York City." *International Migration Review* 29:657-670.

Goldscheider, Frances K. and Calvin Goldscheider. 1993. *Leaving Home Before Marriage: Ethnicity, Familism, and Generational Relationships.*

Gomez-Quinones, Juan. 1994. *Mexican-American Labor, 1790-1990.* Albuquerque, NM: University of New Mexico Press.

Gonzalez de la Rocha, Mercedes. 1994. *The Resources of Poverty: Women and Survival in a Mexican City.* Cambridge, MA: Blackwell.

—. 1995. "The Urban Family and Poverty in Latin America." *Latin American Perspectives* 22:12-31.

—. 2001. "From the Resources of Poverty to the Poverty of Resources? The Erosion of a Survival Model." *Latin American Perspectives* 28:72-100.

Gonzalez-Lopez, Gloria. 2004. "Fathering Latina Sexualities: Mexican Men and the Virginity of Their Daughters." *Journal of Marriage and Family* 66:1118-1130.

Grasmuck, Sherri and Patricia R. Pessar. 1991. *Between Two Islands: Dominican International Migration.* Berkeley: University of California Press.

Guidi, Marta. 1993. "Is Migration Really a Survival Strategy? An Example from the Mixteca Alta Oaxaquena [in Spanish]." *Revista Internacional de Sociologia* 5:89-109.

Health and Migration Survey. 2003. "HOUSFILE96." producer/distributor Rice University, URL: http://www.mexmah.com.

Hirsch, Jennifer S. 2003. *A Courtship after Marriage.* Berkeley and Los Angeles: University of California Press.

Hogan, Dennis P. and David J. Eggebeen. 1995. "Sources of Emergency Help and Routine Assistance in Old Age." *Social Forces* 73:917-936.

Hogan, Dennis P., David J. Eggebeen, and Clifford C. Clogg. 1993. "The Structure of Intergenerational Exchange in American Families." *American Journal of Sociology* 98:1428-1458.

Hondagneu-Sotelo, Pierrette. 1994. *Gendered Transitions: Mexican Experiences of Immigration.* Berkeley and Los Angeles: University of California Press.

—. 2001. *Domestica: Immigrant Workers Cleaning and Caring in the Shadows of Affluence.* Berkeley: University of California Press.

—. 2003. *Gender and U.S. Immigration: Contemporary Trends.* Berkeley and Los Angeles: University of California Press.

Immigration and Naturalization Service. 1997. *Statistical Yearbook of the Immigration and Naturalization Service*. Washington, DC: United States Government Printing Office.

———. 2003. "Estimates of the Unauthorized Immigrant Population Residing in the United States: 1990 to 2000." Office of Policy and Planning, U.S. Immigration and Naturalization Service, Washington, DC.

Jasso, Guillermina, Douglas S. Massey, Mark R. Rosenzweig, and James P. Smith. 2000. "The New Immigrant Survey Pilot (NIS-P): Overview and New Findings about U.S. Legal Immigrants at Admission." *Demography* 37:127-138.

Jasso, Guillermina and Mark R. Rosenzweig. 1990. *The New Chosen People: Immigrants in the United States*. New York: Russell Sage Foundation.

Jones, Richard C. 1998. "Remittances and Inequality: A Question of Migration Stage and Geographic Scale." *Economic Geography* 74:8-25.

Kanaiaupuni, Shawn M. 1995. "The Role of Women in the Social Process of Migration: Household Organizational Strategies of Mexican Families." Sociology, University of Chicago, Chicago.

———. 1999. "Leaving Parents Behind: Migration and Elderly Living Arrangements in Mexico." University of Wisconsin Center for Demography and Ecology, Madison, WI.

Kanaiaupuni, Shawn M. and Katharine M. Donato. 1999. "Migradollars and Mortality: The Effects of Migration on Infant Survival in Mexico." *Demography* 36:339-353.

Kanaiaupuni, Shawn M. and Paula Fomby. 2000. "Men Who Migrate and Women Who Work: Non-Migrant Women and U.S.-Mexico Migration." presented at the annual meeting of the American Sociological Association. Washington, DC.

Kandel, William and Douglas S. Massey. 2002. "The Culture of Mexican Migration: A Theoretical and Empirical Analysis." *Social Forces* 80:981-1004.

Katz, Elizabeth. 1991. "Breaking the Myth of Harmony: Theoretical and Methodological Guidelines to the Study of Rural Third World Households." *Review of Radical Political Economics* 23:37-56.

Latapi, Augustin Escobar, Philip Martin, Gustavo Lopez Castro, and Katharine M. Donato. 1998. "Factors that Influence Migration." Pp. 163-250 in *Migration Between Mexico and the United States: Binational Study*, vol. 1. Mexico City and Washington, DC:

Mexican Ministry of Foreign Affairs and U.S. Commission on
    Immigration Reform.

Lee, Everett S. 1966. "A Theory of Migration." *Demography* 3:47-57.

Lee, Yean-Ju, William L. Parish, and Robert J. Willis. 1994. "Sons,
    Daughters, and Intergenerational Support in Taiwan." *American
    Journal of Sociology* 99:1010-1041.

Lillard, Lee A. and Robert J. Willis. 1997. "Motives for
    Intergenerational Transfers: Evidence from Malaysia."
    Demography 34:115-134.

Lindstrom, David P. and Silvia G. Saucedo. 2002. "The Short- and
    Long-Term Effects of U.S. Migration Experience on Women's
    Fertility." *Social Forces* 80:1341-1368.

Litwak, E. and Charles F. Longino. 1987. "Migration Patterns among
    the Elderly: A Developmental Perspective." *The Gerontologist*
    27:266-272.

Logan, John R. and Glenna D. Spitze. 1995. "Self-Interest and Altruism
    in Intergenerational Relations." *Demography* 32:353-364.

Long, J. Scott. 1997. *Regression Models for Categorical and Limited
    Dependent Variables*. Thousand Oaks, CA: Sage Publications.

Long, J. Scott and Jeremy Freese. 2001. *Regression Models for
    Categorical Dependent Variables Using Stata*. College Station,
    TX: Stata Press.

Lucas, Robert E. B. and Oded Stark. 1985. "Motivations to Remit:
    Evidence from Botswana." *The Journal of Political Economy*
    93:901-918.

Martin, Linda G. and Kevin Kinsella. 1994. "Research on the
    Demography of Aging in Developing Countries." Pp. 356-397 in
    Demography of Aging, edited by L. G. Martin and S. H. Preston.
    Washington, DC: National Academy Press.

Massey, Douglas S., Rafael Alarcon, Jorge Durand, and Humberto
    Gonzalez. 1987. *Return to Aztlan: The Social Process of
    International Migration from Western Mexico*. Berkeley:
    University of California Press.

Massey, Douglas S., Joaquin Arango, Graeme Hugo, Ali Kouaouci,
    Adela Pellogrino, and Edward J. Taylor. 1994. "An Evaluation of
    International Migration Theory: The North American Case."
    Population and Development Review 20:699-751.

Massey, Douglas S., Jorge Durand, and Nolan J. Malone. 2002. *Beyond
    Smoke and Mirrors: Mexican Immigration in an Era of Economic
    Integration*. New York: Russell Sage Foundation.

Massey, Douglas S. and Kristin E. Espinosa. 1997. "What's Driving Mexico-U.S. Migration? A Theoretical, Empirical, and Policy Analysis." *American Journal of Sociology* 102:939-999.

Massey, Douglas S., Luin Goldring, and Jorge Durand. 1994. "Continuities in Transnational Migration: An Analysis of Nineteen Mexican Communities." *American Journal of Sociology* 99:1492-1533.

Massey, Douglas S. and Audrey Singer. 1995. "New Estimates of Undocumented Mexican Migration and the Probability of Apprehensions." *Demography* 32:203-213.

Massey, Douglas S. and Rene M. Zenteno. 2000. "A Validation of the Ethnosurvey: The Case of Mexico-U.S. Migration." *International Migration Review* 34:766-793.

Mexican Migration Project. 2003. "HOUSE, MIG, PERS, LIFE, SPOUSE." producer/distributor Office of Population Research, Princeton University, URL: hhtp://mmp.opr.princeton.edu.

Montes de Oca, Veronica. 1996. "The Third Age: Social Situations of the Elderly (in Spanish)." *Demos* 9:34-35.

—. 2001. "Older adults and their informal support [in Spanish]." *Demos* 14:34-35.

Mutchler, J.E. and J.A. Burr. 1991. "A Longitudinal Analysis of Household and Nonhousehold Living Arrangements in Later Life." *Demography* 28:375-390.

Myrdal, Gunnar. 1957. *Rich Lands and Poor*. New York: Harper and Row.

Nash, John F. 1950. "The Bargaining Problem." *Econometrica* 18:155-162.

Oppenheimer, Valerie Kincaide. 1994. "Women's Rising Employment and the Future of the Family in Industrial Societies." *Population and Development Review* 20:293-341.

Palloni, Alberto, Douglas S. Massey, Miguel Ceballos, Kristin E. Espinosa, and Mike Spittel. 2001. "Social Capital and International Migration: A Test Using Information on Family Networks." *American Journal of Sociology* 106:1262-1298.

Palma, Jose Luis. 2001. "Transfers from and to the older population within and outside of the household [in Spanish]." *Demos* 14:40-41.

Pedraza, Sylvia. 1991. "Women and Migration: The Social Consequences of Gender." *Annual Review of Sociology* 17:303-325.

160

References

Pedraza-Bailey, Sylvia. 1990. "Immigration Research: A Conceptual Map." *Social Science History* 14:43-67.

Pessar, Patricia R. 2003. "Engendering Migration Studies: The Case of New Immigrants in the United States." Pp. 20-42 in *Gender and U.S. Immigration: Contemporary Trends*, edited by P. Hondagneu-Sotelo. Berkeley: University of California Press.

Pezzin, Liliana E. and Barbara S. Schone. 2000. "Intergenerational Transfers and the Distribution of Filial Responsibility for parental care: The Roles of Gender, Family, and Individual Effects." presented at the Annual Meeting of the Population Association of America, Los Angeles.

Piore, Michael J. 1979. *Birds of Passage: Migrant Labor and Industrial Societies*. New York: Cambridge University Press.

Portes, Alejandro. 1995. *The Economic Sociology of Immigration: Essays on Networks, Ethnicity, and Entrepreneurship*. New York: Russell Sage Foundation.

Portes, Alejandro and Robert L. Bach. 1985. *Latin Journey: Cuban and Mexican Immigrants in the United States*. Berkeley: University of California Press.

Sanchez, George J. 1993. *Becoming Mexican American: Ethnicity, Culture, and Identity in Chicano Los Angeles, 1900-1945*. New York and Oxford: Oxford University Press.

Schmink, Marianne. 1984. "Household Economic Strategies: Review and Research Agenda." *Latin American Research Review* 19:87-101.

Selby, Henry A., Arthur D. Murphy, and Stephen A. Lorenzen. 1990. *The Mexican Urban Household: Organizing for Self-Defense*. Austin: University of Texas Press.

Sen, Amartya. 1990. "Gender and Cooperative Conflicts." Pp. 123-149 in *Persistent Inequalities: Women and World Development*, edited by I. Tinker. New York and Oxford: Oxford University Press.

Smith, James P. and Barry Edmonston. 1997. *The New Americans: Economic, Demographic, and Fiscal Effects of Immigration*. Washington, DC: National Academy Press.

Solis, Patricio. 1999. "Living Arrangements of the Elderly in Mexico." in *Annual Meetings of the Population Association of America*. New York.

Stark, Oded and Robert E. B. Lucas. 1988. "Migration, Remittances, and the Family." *Economic Development and Cultural Change* 36:465-481.

Stark, Oded and Edward J. Taylor. 1989. "Relative Deprivation and International Migration." *Demography* 26:1-14.

Taylor, Edward J., Joaquin Arango, Graeme Hugo, Ali Kouaouci, Douglas S. Massey, and Adela Pellegrino. 1996. "International Migration and National Development." *Population Index* 62:181-212.

Thomas, Duncan. 1991. "Like Father, Like Son: Gender Differences in Household Resource Allocations." New Haven, CT: Yale Economic Growth Center.

Todaro, Michael P. 1969. "A Model of Labor Migration and Urban Underemployment in Less Developed Countries." *The American Economic Review* 59:138-148.

Treas, Judith. 1993. "Money in the Bank: Transaction Costs and the Economic Organization of Marriage." *American Sociological Review* 58:723-734.

White, Lynn. 1994. "Coresidence and Leaving Home: Young Adults and Their Parents." *Annual Review of Sociology* 20:81-102.

Williamson, Oliver E. 1979. "Transaction Cost Economics: The Governance of Contractual Relations." *Journal of Law and Economics* 22:233-261.

—. 1981. "The Economics of Organization: The Transaction Cost Approach." *American Journal of Sociology* 87:548-577.

Wolf, Douglas. 1994. "The Elderly and Their Kin: Patterns of Availability and Access." in *Demography of Aging*, edited by L. G. Martin and S. H. Preston. Washington, DC: National Academy Press.

Wolf, Douglas and Beth Soldo. 1988. "Household Composition Choices of Older Unmarried Women." *Demography* 25:387-403.

Wong, Rebeca, Beth J. Soldo, and Chiara Capoferro. 2000. "Generational Social Capital: The Effects on Remittance Streams in Mexico." presented at the Annual Meeting of the Population Association of America, Los Angeles.

Wood, Charles H. 1981. "Structural Changes and Household Strategies: A Conceptual Framework for the Study of Rural Migration." *Human Organization* 40:338-344.

—. 1982. "Equilibrium and Historical-Structural Perspectives on Migration." *International Migration Review* 16:298-319.

INDEX

A

Availability of kin, 59, 60, 63, 72, 77, 81, 88, 89, 102, 146, 147

B

Birth order, 39, 57, 58, 63, 66, 72, 76, 80, 82, 88, 90, 106, 146

E

Earnings transfers, child-to-parent, 1, 2, 3, 8, 9, 12, 18, 28, 29, 31, 34, 36, 54, 102, 122, 123, 125, 134, 135, 139, 143, 148, 150
   motivation, 1, 10, 29, 36, 61, 123, 124, 125, 127, 129, 130, 138, 139, 142, 144, 148, 149
Motivation, 124
Economic need, 23, 58, 59, 60, 63, 64, 66, 67, 71, 72, 77, 80, 83, 88, 89, 90, 91, 101, 103, 109, 130, 131, 146, 147
Dependency ratio, 30, 59, 94, 95, 107, 109, 116, 120, 134
Employment status, 59, 65, 66, 67, 71, 80, 81, 106, 109, 119, 120, 130
Socioeconomic status, 18, 39, 55, 58, 59, 67, 71, 80, 81, 89, 103, 129, 134
Education, 11, 14, 20, 22, 28, 29, 33, 34, 38, 50, 53, 54, 55, 58, 59, 60, 66, 71, 80, 81, 83, 89, 105, 106, 122, 124, 125, 129, 139

F

Female migration, 3, 7, 8, 22

daughters, 3, 62, 66, 76, 83, 88, 142
sisters, 74, 88, 114, 115, 117, 118, 119

H

Health and Migration Survey (HMS), 37, 47, 48, 49, 123, 126, 127, 131
Homeleaving, 11, 72, 93, 94, 96, 102, 103, 104, 105, 106, 107, 109, 118, 119, 120, 121, 147, 148, 149
Household consolidation, 4, 5, 95, 101, 102, 109
Household dispersion, 5, 9, 35, 95, 96, 102, 106, 109, 115, 118, 119, 120

I

Immigration policy, U.S., 3, 5
Immigration Reform and Control Act (IRCA), 7, 20, 22, 68
Intergenerational relations, 1, 4, 5, 9, 35, 95, 96, 101, 102, 106, 109, 115, 118, 119, 120, 146, 151

L

Life course, 35, 59, 89, 94, 102, 103, 105, 106, 109, 114, 118, 120, 123, 150

M

Male migration, 67, 88
   brothers, 74, 82, 90, 116
   sons, 3, 76, 77, 80, 81, 82, 83, 88